Living
in the House
of Drugs

Also by Christine Keleny

Historical Fiction
The Rose Series:
Rosebloom
A Burnished Rose
Rose from the Ashes

Will the Real Carolyn Keene
Please Stand Up

Family Books:
The Red Velvet Box

Intrigue in Istanbul:
An Agnes Kelly Mystery Adventure

LiViNG iN THE HOUSE OF DRUGS

A Memoir of
Willie Triplett

Written by Christine Keleny

CKBooks

The people mentioned in this book are real but their names have been changed.

No parts of this book may be reproduced, scanned, or distributed in any printed or electronic form without permission, except small excerpts for reviews. Contact: CKBooks Publishing, P.O. Box 214, New Glarus, WI, 53574

Follow Christine Keleny on facebook • facebook/ckbooks, twitter • @cmkbooks, blogs • ckbooksblog.wordpress.com or • ckbookspublishing.com/blog/. Find all her books at christinekelenybooks.com

Publisher's Cataloging-In-Publication Data
(Prepared by The Donohue Group, Inc.)

Keleny, Christine.
  Living in the house of drugs : a memoir of Willie Triplett / written by Christine Keleny.

  p. ; cm.

  ISBN: 978-0-9892152-0-6

  1. Triplett, Willie. 2. Recovering addicts--Biography. 3. Recovering alcoholics--Biography. 4. Drug abuse. 5. Biography. I. Title.

HV5805.T75 K45 2013
362.29/092   Library of Congress Control Number: 2013905694

Cover by: Earl Keleny

Copyright © 2013, Christine Keleny
All rights reserved

Printed in the United States
Published by CKBooks Publishing
P.O. Box 214, New Glarus, WI, 53574

I would like to
dedicate this book
to God,
who saved my life.
*
Willie Lee Triplett

Chapter 1
Holy crap

I'm sitting in my car outside the Jamaican restaurant where Willie likes to hang out. We had our first interview here two weeks ago. Willie told me that the owner lets him sleep in the back on occasion.

Willie had been waiting for me here for over an hour, and when I didn't show up, he left. The gentleman at the restaurant said Willie would be back, so I wait. I feel like it's the least I can do. He has already left me six messages on my cell phone telling me that he was waiting for me here. I had already driven a couple blocks down the street to make sure Willie wasn't sitting outside of my brother's rental property where I had picked him up the week before. Willie's first message from last night said he would be sitting there. I wanted to make sure he didn't go back there since I hadn't shown up at the restaurant when I said I would.

The problem is I didn't check my messages again after I received Willie's first message this morning because I knew I couldn't call him back. I was at work and, unfortunately for Willie, I got out late. Willie isn't allowed to have a phone. Drug dealers and users have cell phones, and since Willie is staying in a court-sponsored halfway house after being let out of jail because of a possession charge just three weeks ago, they don't let him have a phone. They also don't let him have more than twenty dollars a week, which pisses Willie off. He doesn't think he can function on twenty dollars a week. Maybe that's supposed to be his motivation to find a job.

You see, Willie has been drinking since he was five and doing drugs since he was seven. Willie has been in a state prison twice, sentenced to three years the first time and six years the second, and just four weeks ago he decided he's had enough. He's had enough of "drinkin' and druggin'," but mostly he's had enough of "losin' things": losing clothes and jewelry, losing cars – "Man, I had some nice cars" – losing money, and I think most important of all to Willie, losing women.

Willie considers himself a ladies' man. He likes women and he likes sex. I find out that it's not that he used sex to get drugs, as he had intimated at our first meeting, but it's the other way around; he used drugs to get sex. Willie has an addiction to having sex while he's high.

Willie Lee Triplett

I am interviewing Willie because Willie has asked me to write his life story. Willie knows I write and have published a couple books of my own, so he wants me to put his thoughts down for him. He says he is doing this so that others can read about his life and learn from his mistakes; he wants to help people so they don't end up like he ended up. At this point, I am taking him at his word. In the short time I have known Willie, I do know that Willie tends to tell it like it is. You can usually tell when Willie is bullshitting you; he's not a very good liar. But his struggle with addiction is just that, a struggle. So I can't help but feel that the other reason he wants to do this is to try and make sense of it all, somehow. Maybe if he tells his story out loud and others read it, it will validate all that he has gone through and continues to go through to try and beat this addiction.

I look out of the windshield of my car, and I catch sight of Willie two car-lengths away. He is standing next to the parked cars in the street. He has on a black stocking cap, a worn plaid jacket, and blue jeans. Willie's about my height – about 5'6" – and a little stocky. Willie likes to eat.

He points to me and gives me his now familiar Willie smile – a sideways sort of wry smile – as he saunters over to my side of the car. If I had known what he was going to tell me in my interview today, after he had reeled off some pretty raunchy, graphic tales as if he was reading off a grocery list – doing as much drugs and having as much sex as he could pay for – I would have contemplated scheduling another appointment with him.

But initially, as I watch that sly smile and that strut, I think it is just Willie being Willie, so I roll down the window. He reaches in and gives me a hug and kiss on the cheek. In the three weeks that I have been working closely with Willie, he's never given me a kiss before. He had always hugged me but never a kiss. I'm momentarily stunned, but I brush it off, as I try to do with most things with Willie.

Willie frequently does things I am not particularly comfortable with: the language he may use, the physical closeness he likes to have, the looks he gives me at times. He grew up in the projects in Chicago. I grew up in a predominately white, middle-class city. His role models were black hustlers, mine were white liberals. He barely made it through school, I have a college degree. So I expect to be surprised at times by what Willie says or does. But so far, it's all been minor things, so I let the peck on the cheek pass without a comment. I've got my guard up more than usual, ready to deflect anything else he tries in that direction. I don't expect anything, but who knows.

I let him in the passenger side of the car so we can go somewhere to start our interview. He's got to be back at the halfway house by three and it's almost two.

"What's up, cupcake? How you doin'?"
I bristle.
"You don't like dat nick name?" he asks.
"Not really. I don't really consider myself a cupcake," I reply.

"Dat's a good thing?" he says, trying to convince me otherwise. He can tell I don't go for it. "How 'bout pumpkin?" he offers as a substitution.

"That's better, but don't say it when anyone else is around," I instruct him.

I don't mind if he wants to adopt me like some sort of puppy by giving me a nickname, but I'd rather he keep it between the two of us.

We decide we'll go to the library just a mile or so from his halfway house, where we had gone the week before. That location had worked out fairly well. We had been told to quiet down only once, but we didn't get kicked out. Willie informs me he has to get a paper signed by a local business first, then check in at the halfway house before we can start our conversation.

One of the requirements for Willie to live in this halfway house is he has to get five signatures a day, to show he's been looking for a job. He has to leave at eight a.m. and be back no later than four p.m. So we drive a couple blocks to a pay phone (he can't use my cell phone or he'll get in trouble) and down another block to an ice-cream place. Willie will have them sign his preapproved job sheet.

As fate would have it, they have an empty room for us to use at the library. So we settle in, me at my computer, Willie sitting sideways on the bench next to me so he can see what I'm writing.

Today I want to get something for the beginning of

the book, so I tell him I want him to talk about his lowest point, or the point where he had decided he had had enough of drinking and drugs. It turns out they weren't the same thing. I didn't know how much sex played a part in Willie's addictions, but I soon would.

(It is sometime in the 1990s, Chicago, Illinois. Willie is thirty-seven)

"I was on the corner of Sherman and Lawrence Street standin' by the Sherman Hotel. It was pourin' down rain. A white guy pulls up and says, 'You wanna turn a date? If you let me go down on you, I'll give you fifty dollars.'

"I hadn't gotten high in like three days, so I don't think about it too long, so I got in his car. He took me to his house, and we go down into the basement. Then without expectin' it, he pulled a sword on me. He wants me to go down him. I did it. Den he told me, screw him. Now I was confused. I didn't know what to do. I hadn't screwed no man before, but I wanted the fifty dollars, so I screwed 'im. I didn't get off, but he got off. He paid me my money, den he put me out of his house in the pourin' down rain. I was standin' in the rain thinkin' I should'a robbed 'im. But he might'a called the cops. Dat was the first time I thought, 'What's wrong with me?'

"I came upon a lady [a whore]. I tol' her what went down. She said it's hard the first time you do somethin' like dat. When you get bad, you'll do more den dat. We became hustlin' partners. I did the day [for drugs], she did the night [for money]. I got comfortable with druggin' every day."

Here comes the grocery list. He goes from one story to the next and tells me these embarrassing, amazing stories so fast it's as if he has to get them off of his chest. He has to tell me all the eye-popping details so I know how bad it was, so everyone will know how bad it was. He doesn't leave much out, and I'm glad I'm looking at the computer screen and not at Willie as he tells me about this next encounter.

"It was around dis same time. I came upon a guy, and the man ax for a girl. [Willie assumes the man wants a girl so he can have sex with her.] Dis guy wants to get high. Dis is 1992 at seven to eight at night. I find a girl and we go with him together. When we get to his apartment, I find out he's gay. He had a mirror and a stool in the middle of the floor. We all get high. His sex drive gets high as he gets high. He wants to see me have sex with the girl as he watches in the mirror. Den we all take a hit. He wants me to blow smoke up her vagina, and I did dat and the girl did dat to me, too. He would smoke, and he would get off as he watched us have sex."

Even though Willie tells me he likes getting high and having sex, at this point in his life he admits to himself that he was getting a little crazy. So after he hadn't had any drugs for a few days he went to a place called Chicago Uptown Ministry.

Willie had been living on the street, so he was dirty and he smelled, but they let him in. They let him shower, gave him some clean clothes, and fed him. He remembers three different men that worked at this ministry: the pastor, a man named Dave, and a black man by the name of Charlie. Charlie tells him something he has never thought of before: He doesn't have to look like a bum to be homeless.

Willie liked the Uptown Ministry, so he went there every day. He soon realized that he had to stop getting high, but, of course, he didn't. He actually got caught stealing something and landed in jail

When Willie got out of jail he went into a six-month rehab program. He even went to a worldwide AA (Alcoholic Anonymous) convention. But, as he put it, "I still be messin' with the girls," and he falls off the wagon and goes on a three-day binge.

At this point he realized he messed up, and he tried to get back into the six-month program again. They referred him to another program, a drug rehabilitation program, but he continued to use, and he was getting more desperate.

"I was on Lawrence and Broadway. A white guy come up in a yellow Corvette. He has a pregnant wife. He took out two or three thousand dollars to get dope. He ax me, can I get him some dope. See, a white guy can't ax for dope hisself, he has to ax a black guy to get it for 'im. He give me three hundred dollars to see if I'd come back with the dope. I went to the twin towers to get the dope.

"When you go up to the twin towers, the guys come out sayin' dey can get you the dope. You don't even have to go in lookin' for it. I got the dope, so we went someplace to get high. Den we went and got a girl. We went to the basement of an abandoned buildin' and got high. He said we all have to get naked. We was doing everythin'. There were two womens – both white – and dis white guy and me. When the white boy run outta money, he lent his Corvette out to the dealer to get more dope.

"He called his wife to bring him another thousand dollars. She brought it. She axed him where his car is. He said he lent it out. He didn't tell her he lent it to a dope dealer. He called again for another thousand dollars. She came about five times to dis abandoned buildin'. We were in dere three ta four days gettin' high and havin' sex. The last time he was scared to call her. Dis time she didn't bring no money, she came but she was mad. She walked off.

"I didn't care. I just wanted to get high.

"Dis is where God came in.

"I told her, 'Your husband's down here in the basement. If you love your husband, I'm gonna take you down in the basement. You take him home. Get him some help. If I see him down here again, it ain't gonna be the same.'

"I take her down dere and it's a mess, shit and piss all around. She's cryin'. Dey left. Dey didn't come around no more."

This is a disturbing story to be sure and I'm amazed how easily he can tell it, but I don't really stop tapping my fingers on the keys until Willie tells me this next bit.

"I'm in dis club and dis dope dealer had two hundred dollars worth'a rocks [rocks of crack cocaine] in his mouth, [ten – twenty-dollar bags]. The police raid the club so dis guy swallowed the rocks. The guy goes to a restaurant to get some food. He ate and he drank somethin', den he threw it all up. He didn't want the rocks no more. He said I could have 'em. I got down on my knees and picked 'em all up."

Holy Crap! I think to myself. *How does a person get that low?*

It's hard for me to imagine this, coming from my lily-white neighborhood with my lily-white friends, where the worst thing we did when we were young was sneak a few cigarettes or try to choke down some of our parent's hard liquor.

Willie then proceeds to tell me that he finds a girl and tells her he will give her a couple of these rocks of cocaine if she will have sex with him. So they proceed to get high and have sex.

Sometime during all this Willie goes to prison for stealing stuff out of cars. When he gets out of prison a year and a half later (with a year and a half parole), something happens that disturbs him deeply, and I can tell that it still stings.

"When I get outta prison, I found out my momma

started smokin' cocaine. I really, really didn't like dat. She had a couple friends over, and we all got high, and I had sex with 'em. Den my momma axed me to go down on dis gay guy. Dat's when I started cursin' God."

You might be wondering, after I get done hearing all these unabashed accounts of his life on the streets, why I wouldn't be running in the other direction. Well, it's because of Willie. Not because he says he is trying to pick himself up and get off the hamster wheel of relapse and recovery and relapse... I would like to help him with that, of course, but it's because of Willie himself. To use a prosaic though apt metaphor, Willie is like a magnet; he just seems to attract people. You can tell when you meet Willie that he is unique; he has this infectious smile, this personality that, somehow, makes you want to help him, or at minimal, root for him.

I think it is because people are able to tell, from the first time they meet him, that he is sincere. Despite the slick, put-together persona he tries to pull off, Willie is the real deal.

Don't get me wrong, Willie likes to spread the bull, to get away with anything and everything he can if you let him, that's just Willie's style. But underneath all that you can tell there is person who really does care, and once he's taken you into his tribe, he'll fight for you until the last man is down.

As we leave the library, I ask Willie if he thinks he is going to make it, if he thinks he is going to be able to stay straight.

"Well, I can't tell you 'bout tomorrow, only thing I know about is taday."

I know that's the twelve-step program talking, not Willie. Willie has been through the twelve steps on numerous occasions, so I am left to wonder.

Chapter 2

Our First Official Meeting

"Willie, I can't use this," I say as I hold up the six or so pages of hand-written papers – written front and back – for him to see.

Willie had given these papers to my brother, who then mailed them to me with the cryptic note: Willie Triplett's life story.

My brother has known Willie for a couple years now. In fact, he's the one who introduced Willie to me over a year ago. He hires Willie on occasion to help him with some manual labor – the kind of work Willie is good at and likes to do.

Some of Willie's story that I have in my hand is written on white lined paper, some on yellow note-pad paper. Every other page or so is in a different handwriting, mostly printed with very little punctuation and no breaks on the page, just continuous words. When I got it, I just skimmed the first page, so I didn't catch the fact that Willie probably hadn't written any of this himself, and in his Willie sort of way – you'll understand what I mean by this as we go along here – he had dictated this for others to write down for him. I showed these pages to a fellow writer who clued me in on this small detail, a detail that would greatly impact how this whole book writing process was going to go. At the moment, I had no idea what I was in for.

We sit across from each other in a booth at a Chinese restaurant. Willie wanted to have lunch. I suggested McDonald's; Willie had other ideas. Willie tells me that he graduated from high school, a fact he is obviously proud of, but from these pages, it appears that he has minimal writing skills, and, I would guess, minimal reading skills, as well.

"I need you to enter this into a computer," I tell him.

"I don't have no computer."

"You can go to the library to use one. I'll have to get you a thumb drive; a little thing that you use to save what you've typed up. We can probably get it at Shopko," I say, pointing to the strip mall next to the restaurant we're sitting in.

"I don't know how ta type."

"It's not that hard. You just use a couple fingers," I say, holding up my two index fingers and pretend I'm doing the hunt and peck method of typing on a keyboard. "I can show you. I've got time this afternoon," I say enthusiastically, hoping I can convince him of his ability to do this.

I just don't have the time right now to type up these pages for him that, at best, were going to be difficult to translate. I am up to my eyeballs in projects. I am working part-time, trying to finish up my second book, and trying to work on new marketing strategies for the new audio version of my first book. On top of all that, my brother and I have been kicking around the idea of publishing a children's book we had put together over ten years ago.

Willie is very eager to get his book going, and I am willing to help, but he needs to help me do this. I keep an upbeat voice and continue my sell job.

"I've checked, there's a library in your area that you can go to to do the typing, then save what you've typed on that thumb drive."

Willie hesitates and looks down at the table for a brief second then looks back up at me with a wry, Willie, smile.

"Yeah, okay I guess."

I can tell he's still not convinced, but he's willing to see what I can show him.

"Why don't you go get your lunch," I encourage him, before he talks himself out of my grand typing experiment. "We can talk more while you eat."

Willie opens the door for me as we leave the restaurant as he did when we had entered. I tease him about the gentlemanly gesture.

"You're quite a smooze, Willie."

He smiles at me with that sideways Willie smile.

"Somebody has to," he says playfully.

Then he automatically picks up his youthful swagger as he recounts his high school days, how he and his friends would dress up real nice and impress the girls. It comes back to him easily – this swagger – though I doubt he's employed it on anyone lately other than his counselors, or other people like me whom he is trying to get something from. And don't be mistaken; Willie is always trying to get something from someone. It's second nature to him. He is so used to doing this he doesn't even ask for favors, he just tells you where he needs to go or what he needs you to get him, and he hopes you don't question him. He hasn't asked me for something I'm not willing to supply so far, but my guess is that's coming.

As we drive closer to the library, he wants to show me some of the places he has been to in this neighborhood, the places he had used, the places he had gotten drunk.

"Go down dis way," he says, pointing to our left. Again, telling instead of asking.

The houses and apartments he points out to me are pretty nondescript, but I could tell they have meaning to Willie. They were part of his life and, as I come to know Willie, a part he sincerely hopes is history.

I actually knew this neighborhood myself. I had gone to middle school there, so I knew something about it. It was a rough part of town when I went to school there, and I knew it still was but probably more so. Willie continues my education even as we pull into our parking stall in front of the library by pointing out some "hustlers" [drug dealers] with a couple other young men that walk by our car.

"You can tell by the clothes he got on, dey got nice clean shoes, new clothes. Dey crisp," he explains.

We walk into a different library than the one in the area where he presently lives. We are in a library in the neighborhood Willie used to haunt when he was using. It's the closest one to the Chinese restaurant and closer to the place he is presently working, cleaning out a basement of someone's home. He also has a meeting in this same area around five p.m., so he didn't want to go to the library by his halfway house. (Five p.m. is past his curfew, but it's really none of my business, so I don't mention it.)

We sit by an unoccupied computer. It's unoccupied, we come to find out, because it doesn't have Internet access. Which is fine for us, we only need a computer with a writing program. Well, it does have a writing program, but after we try and save our sample document on Willie's new, lime-green thumb drive, as the librarian said we could, it doesn't work. A different librarian explains that you can't save documents with that program, you have to use the program on the computers that have Internet access, which, of course, are all still in use.

We are also told that you have to have a library or

Internet card to get on an Internet computer. I already know from Willie that he can't get a library card. He tried to get a card once, at the main library downtown, and they wouldn't give it to him because of an old fine he has yet to pay at a library in the Chicago area. He tells this to me with a chuckle in his voice, tinged with a touch of embarrassment.

I ask the librarian if Willie can get an Internet card, then Willie sheepishly goes into his library card story for the librarians who look at this black man with a missing front tooth and this white woman standing next to him, with questioning eyes. I know these ladies have seen a lot and heard most every library story and excuse one can imagine – this is a library that you are either sent to or volunteer to go to; no one would choose to work in this library – so they don't look at us long, they just listen patiently and assure us he can get an Internet card. Luckily, this time they're right. Another hurdle mounted! But will he type? Will he be able to read the large print, cursory directions I have written down for him that we practiced in the library that afternoon?

Two days later I get my answer. It's a message from Willie on my cell phone.

"Hey, dis is Willie," he says in an upbeat tone, then his voice changes slightly. "I spent two hours at the library yesterday. Dat typin' thing's harder than you said, but I did it. I just wanted to let you know. I heard what you said 'bout not wastin' your time. I don't want to waste my time neither, so I'll keep workin' on dis."

He pauses briefly, probably not sure how to end a conversation with a white woman who isn't from his neighborhood.

"I'll be talkin' at ya later. God bless ya, now."

Here's what Willie wrote after three trips and six hours at the library computer:

THIS is my STORY

I was born in 1962 . I born in Jackson Mississippi ; my mother name is Rose Lee TRIPLETT. we moving to Chicago to the west side of Chicago we were live on warren st I remember when I was a child I see my mother do something and didn't understand don't know. I knew I had a problem In my house . when I was a child and I saw my mother get dressed I assumed she was going out to party. Live in a house when no heat . I see my mother come home when a man I did not know him he and my mother when in to a room when him .I don't know what happened I remember when I was a kid my mother got married to a man name MACK LUMPKINS. he was a nice dad to me . then she get pregnant . then hed baby. Then have 3 kid. then 2.more. I don't remember why they broke up. THIS is my FAMILY name in my mother house . Bernice; Rosemarie SENDOR Charles POPDADDY I remember my sister got burned on her feet.

> *welfare came and took us from my mother then we went to a foster home. Then my mother got us back we moving to project we were living in a project Apartment on western van Buren on the for 4 floor. I went to SCHOOL around neighborhood I knew I had a problem Live in the project . THE name of the project is rock well gardens .. I remember i took a bike and I run into a pole and my nose start to bleed .then lef the bike went home to mother my and crying . I knew I had a problem live in project and seed gangs run around the neighbor .66666".*

I asked Willie why he put the sixes at the end of his writing. He told me he put the five sixes at the end so he knew where he had left off.

Chapter 3
The Beginning

~~~~~~

Willie was just an infant when his momma moved him from Jackson, Mississippi to the first home that he remembers on Warren Street in Chicago. She was eighteen when Willie was born. They lived on the bottom floor of a two-flat house in an all-black neighborhood on Chicago's South side.

When I was asking Willie about Warren Street, the neighborhood, the school... I kept trying to determine if he would come in contact with anyone there who wasn't black. He finally told me, "You can stop askin' me if anyone else lived dere dat wasn't black. Dey was all black."

They were all black except for the police and the social workers who came and took him and his siblings away.

As we are talking, Willie points out a little tidbit of information.

"Siblings. I didn't used to know what dat word was until a couple years ago. We call 'em brothers and sisters, not like the words you white folks use, no offence," he tells me, as he taps me lightly on the leg.

The apartment his family lived in had two rooms and a bath; the main room had a kitchen and living area and was separated by two sliding doors from the bedroom. Willie doesn't remember his daddy being there, just his step dad, Mack Lumpkins, whom he considered his father. As he mentioned in his typing attempt, Mack was very nice to him and treated him like his other three children. I don't think Willie understood the significance of this until he was older and he realized that Mack didn't have to treat him like his own, but he did.

Willie's step-brother and sisters, Sendor, Bernice, and Rose Marie, were all born to Willie's mother and Mack when they lived on Warren Street.

What Willie remembers most about Warren Street is how cold it was. They didn't have hot water or heat. They lived in this house until he was seven or eight.

But as insignificant as it seems to Willie as he relates his early childhood to me, Warren Street was where he was first introduced to alcohol and marijuana, and where he first stole something. Though the first time Willie stole something it wasn't because he needed it to sell for drugs, it was the more typical child's innocent attempt at leveling the playing field.

"When we lived on Warren Street was the first time I

stole somethin'. Now I call it borrowin'. I was six or seven at the time. I was walkin' home from school one day, and I saw dis bike sittin' next to a fence. I'd seen dis bike befo'. The kid dat owned it lived across the street from me. I didn't know 'im, but I knew he and his brothers and sisters had lots a stuff to play with 'cause when dey was done playin' with somethin', dey'd just leave it sit outside in deir yard. I didn't have all the stuff dat boy had, so I figured he wouldn't miss dat bike too much.

"I looked at the house, and I looked up and down the street. No one's around, so I jumped on and started ridin' as fast as I can. I was just thinkin'a gettin' away as fast as I could, lookin' back to make sure no one seen me and was comin' after me. I saw the corner comin' up, and I knew I was almost home free. I started to make the turn, but I turned 'round ta check one more time if I'm gonna make it without gettin' caught, and, BAM, when I turn back around, I run into a green light pole. I thought I done busted my nose. I was bleedin' all over my shirt. I started to cry.

"I forgot all about the bike, and I went home, just across the street. My Mamma said, 'Boy, what's wrong which you? Why is your nose bleedin'?'

"I tol' her I fell. She didn't ax me no more 'bout dat.

"When we lived on Warren was when I learned dat I was a slow learner. The teacher in my grade school was a young lady, and she was real nice. She tried to teach me things in school, but it was hard. She told me to have my momma help me with my homework, but my momma couldn't help me. She could hardly read or write herself, so I just didn't do it.

"It was also where I started to drink. I think I was 'bout five at the time. My Uncle Robert, he'd give me and my brother Sendor, who was just three, money and sips a beer if we danced for 'im. My brother was always better than me at dancin'."

When Willie was six or seven, they moved to a house on Octesha in the same neighborhood. "I don't know how dat's spelled," he told me. (Neither do I!) On Octesha they lived in a three-flat, on the third floor. Willie remembers his mother having family dinners there every Sunday night. His mother would make fried chicken, greens, and corn bread.

His momma also told him to wash his hands after he ate. One night he forgot. I don't think Willie ever forgot again to wash his hands after eating.

"She always told us to wash our hands after we ate. Dat time I didn't. My hand was hangin' over the side of the bed when I was sleepin'. A rat bit my finger, almost to the bone. My momma called the hospital and told dem a rat bit my son. We went to the county hospital. [He can't remember how they got there]. Dey fixed it up.

"The welfare people came and turned the house upside down. Dey found the rat and figured out it didn't have rabies. Dat would'a been bad if it had rabies."

Octesha was where Willie has his first major encounter with law enforcement and Chicago's social system. It's the late sixties. Strangely enough, what seems most significant to Willie about this encounter was how it started.

"We go to the next-door neighbor and steal deir food. I don't know what my momma did with her money? She was on the welfare. I don't remember if my momma worked. I'm not really for sure. She told me she was a dancer one time, but I don't really know. She might'a done dat. She didn't have no boyfriend, some guy friends, but when the family came over, she would dance with 'em to fast music like Diana Ross, The Supremes, OJ's, Spinners, Whispers, Isly Brothers, The Dells, Marvin Gay, Al Green. Dat man could knock dem womens to deir boots. Every one of dem used to love dat man!

"It's winter and dere's snow on the ground. I took a butter knife and got the next door neighbor's door open. We got hot dogs and chicken out of the frig. I handed stuff to my sisters and brother. Den we cooked it up back home. The people next door didn't come home right away, but when dey did, the food was all gone. We were sittin' around talkin' and laughin' back home.

"We didn't get caught, but dey knew it was us: me [Willie is ten], Bernice who's eight or nine [Bernice is no longer living], Rose Marie who's six or seven [he calls her Rhea] and Sendor who's three or four. The neighbors called the cops. The cops came over.

"I was scared. My mamma said, 'don't talk to the police. Don't open the door.' Dey said dey would bust the door down. I opened the door prob'bly 'cause I knew it was wrong, what we did. Dey ax alotta questions: Where's your mamma? Where's your daddy? 'We don't have no daddy.' 'Do you know where your momma went?'

"I was answerin' all the questions. The others were just sittin' very still, very quiet. Before the cops came in I told 'em, 'don't say anythin'. I remember dey had blue uniforms on with a badge and a gun.

"The cops took us to McDonald's and bought us all somethin' to eat, with drinks and everythin'. The cops left a paper at the apartment tellin' my momma where we was, and momma and FC Lumpkins [her boyfriend at the time, Mack FC Lumpkins] came to the station. FC Lumpkins was a truck driver. He made good money. But my momma was lookin' for a man be there moe [more]. She married him, but I ain't sure why dey broke up.

"The Cops put us in a room by ourselves. The welfare people, a man and a lady – dey're white – come with us. I didn't know any better to ask about my mamma. Back den black people be scared of dem whites.

"Dey kept us two months. Momma had to go to court. Dey said she was an unfit parent.

"After FC Lumpkins came and got us from welfare, he got us some clothes. He got me some boxers. He had married her. [Willie's mother]. He know who my dad was. Dey knew each other. Dey lived in the same neighborhood as kids. He was just a nice guy. We'd sit around and watch TV like a family. I call him my dad. He died of a stroke. He gave me fifty dollars the last time I saw him."

Then Willie starts to tell me about his Uncle and the significant role he plays in Willie's life.

"My uncle's named Robert. I was about six or seven. My brother was about four. My uncle tell us to dance. He'd give us beer and a funny cigarette. My momma didn't like dat. 'Don't be givin' the kids none a dat crap,' she'd say. He smoke dis funny cigarette, den give me a little beer. He laughin' at me, makin an ass outta me.

"My mamma already smoked and sold weed. Dey used to sit around the house dancin', partyin'. Dey come to our door in our project. Dey'd sit in the kitchen and she'd bring dem somethin'. I didn't know what it was.

"Den I found a weed stash. I took a little, and I'd smoke it with my friends. [Willie was about ten or twelve years old.]

"When she did find out, she didn't woop me, she spanked me. Den I started buyin' it on the street with my allowance. My allowance was my movie money, too. We'd go way down the hall at home and smoke a joint.

"When I was about fifteen, my momma say, 'I know you smokin' weed. I know you stealin' my stuff. I don't want you smokin' in the house. You smoke it out dere.'

"I really got into it. Lina my cousin. We'd sit around and smoke weed, and we'd listen to Queen – *We Are the*

Champions. Her mom was a hippie. Her mom had a white boyfriend. Dat's the first time I seen it [a mixed racial couple]. He was a cool guy. Dat's when I got into heavy drugs: black beauty, acid, speed. Lina got me into dat. Lina used to come over to our house once a week. She got me hooked on roller skates, too."

"Would you pay her for the drugs?" I asked.

"She had money. She got an allowance. I wasn't buyin' it on my own.

"It seemed like it was the coolest thing to do 'cause your whole family was doin' it, playin' cards, playin' biz wiz or spades, smokin' weed. Dat was cool."

Chapter 4
High School

(This is an unedited letter Willie wrote and dictated while in jail).

> I had friend name Billy Baby. I like the sister and cousin and they are my best friend now. I remember my uncle get me beer I like the taste. I remember I went with a friend and we get drunk and t[h]rew up and I have picke and segram-gin. *[Someone else starts to write past this point].* My mother didn't approve of my uncle giving me things to drink. She used to holler at him all the time. As I got older I realized that drinking and drugging were a way of life. It gave me a picture of the way the world protraid it as a good thing.

Being a kid I thought that drinking and drugging was everything. As a kid growing up in the projects everything seemed glamorized. My cousin was a pimp who always had nice clothes, cars, and women. When I was young I knew he was doing drugs, but I did not know how heavy into drugs he was. Speed and cocaine were an everyday thing for him. He used his pimping to help support his habit. As I grew older I started going to different parties and night clubs, wearing my hair permed and calling myself a hustler. I watched a lot of old movies and saw myself as the stars from movies such as the mack. I found myself hanging out in clubs like hamlen house, King club, Ronnies steak house or my best times at Rainbow skating ring w(h)ere I would get some Bacardi Rum have some Black Beauties and 1/4 bag of weed the go skating with the women. One particular time I came home and my mother had a pot of chitlen on. I burned the whole pot. I remember my mother getting so mad she tied me down with an extension cord and she said she was going to woop me til I bled to death. Soon after I borrowed $30 from my friend Norman G's father to buy some more chitlens to cook myself. That was when I sharted paying more attention to how to cook foods.

Growing up me and Norman G used to smoke

a lot of marajauna and sihkey sticks. Lina my cousin used to come by my house a lot when I was around 15 or 16. We would love to get high on marijauna and listen to Linas all time favorite song "We are the Champions" by Queen. Living in the projects I had a lot of friends. There was one friend in particular named Fred who always rode an old time bicycle. We called him "Slick Fred". Growing up in the projects there were a lot of girls that I was interested in, but being the good guy that I was and not acting like a thug or showing out in front of them, they never seemed to notice me.

I remember one particular time when I was about a sophomore in high school. I was starting to dress better and change my appearance to click more with the guys and impress more of the ladies. On one particular day a girl from my building called me out in front of all my friends and I knew right then that I had to save face in front of everyone. So I promised her a wooping after school. The end of school came and I slapped her around a little bit as promised. But little did I know soon after she would run and tell her mother who know my mother. They both got together and talked about it. Then they talked to me. They explained a lot to me. I think thats when I realy started to understand women more. Just because she said that I learned it didn't realy mean that she didn't like me. She was just showing out in front of her friends the same way I was doing by having to slap her around. It took some time for us both to come to the understanding of what was realy going on in our adolencent puberty drive heads, but soon after we did we became good friends.

Going to church every Sunday was a normal thing growing up in the projects. But there was one particular woman who's family seemed extremely strong. She was always passing the word of God along and helping out in the community. Even though I knew about God prior to that. It was then when I realy started to undersand what religion was realy about. Only then was I truly able to let God into my life.

On[c]e around the age of 16 my cousin come over and we tried to go get some weed from the next project. This project was different turf. It was a GD turf. When we were on the elevator. One of the guys from that project stopped the elevator on us and demaned for us to give him all of our money. I told him to get us unstuck and I would give it to him. But when the elevator got back down, my cousin ran like hell. That gave me no choice but to run to. Once I made it home I got my uncle and all of his friends. We then proceeded to go back and find this guy that tried to rob me of my money.

After I graduted high school, I stayed in my mothers house for one more year. But that's when my cousin Sammy and I got into some trouble. We robbed someone. But when I good samaratein came to the aid of our victim I hit him with my belt buckle and knocked all his teeth out. After that I ran, but a taxi driver had already called the police and proceeded to chase me. I ran as fast as I could but before I knew it I was surround by the police. Then I went to 26 and Califormia County Jail in Chicago.

Willie adds a bit more information about his high school days during one of our meetings. Willie seems like a regular high schooler growing up in a poor neighborhood in Chicago.

"High school was like dis. I used to hang out with dese guys named Billy and Bobby and June. June was a Vise Lord. He was a sharp dresser. We were in a gang dat dressed nice and hang out. I went to basketball and football games. I was in a special ed class. We all came from Grant grade school, then Mckinley seven through nine grades. We all knew each other. We had alotta dancin' parties at Mckinley. Den Crane Tech – a high school and technical school.

"Stuff started goin' on when I was a junior. Misses

Dougen – she was a white woman – she got us into the auto show. I like'ded Misses Dougen. She was nice.

"I remember dis one time. Dere was dis girl dat jumped in the pool, and she couldn't swim. I saved her life. I thought I'd get somethin' outta dat, but I didn't.

"When I was a freshman, I was smokin' weed. We went behind Grant school to smoke after and durin' school. Dey didn't care. We didn't smoke cigarettes but we smoked weed in the bathroom, too.

"After school I'd hang out with my friends. We'd play basketball, football, and squakam. It a game with a square box with an X in a circle. Ya have a pitcher dat throws and two guys out behind the pitcher. You used a rubber ball. We'd get some beer while we played. I drank Schlitz Malt Liquor. It was fun.

"My momma used to know a guy who owned a store, and I'd work dere on the weekend for a little spendin' money.

"My momma would get one thousand dollars a month for the welfare. She'd give me one hundred.

"Sometimes I'd get in a fight at school. Dere was dis dude named Andrew. Andrew lived in the Hendren Hornet [apartments] and I lived in the Rockwell projects. He was a GB – Ganster Black, and I was a Vise Lord. We used to get to fightin' dem guys every day: me, Bobby, Andrew, and Billy. Dey didn't allow us to come over to deir place. We liked deir girls and dey liked our girls. We'd fight every day. There was shootin' and knives. When you get outta school, dere was always fights.

"Sometimes I had to get my uncle to get me back in school.

"We used to break into lockers to steal things: money, watches, stuff like dat. We done never take nobody's clothes. Once dis dude took my leather jacket. I saw him with it on. I said, 'Dat's my jacket.' He said, 'I'm sorry. I didn't know.' He took my jacket off and gave it back to me. Dat's how it was. You done never take each other's clothes.

"One Friday night we had a dance at school in the gym. The gym had a track hangin' around it. We used to skate up dere. I used to step a lot. Steppin' is like doin' the salsa. I asked Ann if she wanted to step with me. She said I can't step; I can't step in my boots. She hurt my feeling real bad, so I learned how ta step. Den I learned the bop. Girls like'ded either, but if you knowed both, den you get the good girls. I always like to flirt and see how the girls react. Boy, dem girls could roller skate, shakin' deir booty.

"When I was a junior, I was well known. I was Will Kill, or Willie D – dynomite, or Trip. All dese names mean you bein' somethin' you not. Everybody had a nickname.

"I was in high school when I got a job at Adam's Food Store and Liquor. First time I worked for him he was diggin' a hole, doin' some plumbin'. He was an A-rab. I say, 'You need some help?' 'Yeah, I need some help.' Dat's when I like'ded plumbin'. He paid me fifty [dollars] a week. Den after a year, he gave me a thirty dollar raise. Pam was workin' the cash register. She was a thief. She didn't take much – thirty to forty every day.

"He used to give me groceries to take home: milk, candy, diapers. He'd take it outta my check on Fridays. I got to know his two kids. He son was an A-rab, and he come over here and start workin' with me. He had another store, too.

"I did stockin' groceries, filled the cooler with water, beer, pop, milk, do inventory, clean the bathrooms. I'd make sure nobody stealin'. I'd keep the place clean. I worked hard.

"I didn't do heavy drugs 'cause I was in stylish people. I always dressed nice, though. It was all about hangin' out and goin' with the girls.

"I like'ded school. I liked to dress, and I like'ded the girls.

"When I was a senior, I met Shanita. She had four sisters. All four got raped in the elevator in the projects. I like'ded her. She let me walk her home, but she didn't give me the time a day. Dey lived in the soul [Black Soul] buildin'. I had an auntie live in dat buildin' and my cousins. [The Black Soul (BS) was a gang that lived in the building and hung out there. Other gangs had other buildings.] One of my cousins was a BS. He had a reputation. He had twenty guys up under him. Dey'd see me come in the buildin'. I'd come in and say hey to my cousin. Dat's the reason how I got to see Shanita, through the grape vine. He was a really bruiser. He beat on her and she had kids by him. Womens like rough neck boys.

"When I was a senior, dat's when I got into jail the first time. You have alotta time to think."

Willie Lee Triplett

Willie didn't really have a particular plan for himself after high school and getting arrested for robbery and battery didn't necessarily help him, but I don't think his prison time set him up to be an addict.

Chapter 5

First Prison Time in Illinois - Joliet/Pontiac

~~~~~~

I pull up into the driveway of the rental property Willie and my brother are working on.

"Hey Willie."

"How you doin', pumpkin," he says with his usual wry smile.

"I'm good. What you boys up to?"

"Oh, we done already. We can go anytime you like."

"That's fine," I say as Willie walks away to get his bicycle. I converse with my brother until Willie comes back.

In his usual Willie style, he walks it up to my car without asking if we can take it along. And without skipping a beat, I fold down the back seats and help him stuff it in the back of my small car.

I say goodbye to my brother and we're off, I know not where.

"So where we heading to?" I ask.

"I have ta get a check from a guy uptown, den we can go wherever you want, pumpkin."

Willie always says "pumpkin" with a little lilt in his voice. It gets to me like nails on a chalk board, but, of course, I ignore it. Willie's flirting, as usual.

I drive Willie to a place uptown and suggest we go to the library just a couple blocks away, and he agrees. We chat about this and that, but I can tell Willie just isn't himself today. My first impression is that he's tired. I find out later I'm partially right, he has been having trouble sleeping.

When we get set up in the library, Willie starts talking to me about his time in prison.

"When you wrote me, you told me about your time in prison. Was that your first time?"

"I went to prison in September 1982. I got arrested for robbery. We had robbed a man. As we was gettin' away, the man called for help. Me and my cousin, Sammy, we ran. We splitted up. He got caught about thirty minutes before I did. So dey found me runnin' down Clark Street going toward South. A cab driver saw what happened and started helpin' the guy we robbed. He seen me, and he started chasin' me

House of Drugs

with his car, and he got out. He was gonna hold me for the po-lice. I took my belt buckle out and hit 'im and knocked his teeth out. Dey got me for robbery and battery. I go to Belmont and Weston [Police Station]. Dey give me a bond outta your reach, so dey shipped me to Twenty-sixth and California [Street Police Station] in a paddy wagon.

"We all in the bull pen, all crowded, smellin' bad. We all standin' around waitin' to get searched. You got two bull pens like dis. The toilet over deir. People everywhere, all kinds of people.

"Dey tell us to get out, three hundred guys in a line, linin' along a wall, and den another line a guys. Dey tell you to take off all your clothes includin' your drawers. People stinkin' drunk, throwin' up.

"So now everyone naked as a jay bird. So den everyone was to bend over and spread deir cheeks den cough."

(The prisoners have to do this to make sure they haven't put something...well let's just say, where the sun doesn't shine.)

"Ninety-five percent are African American black men, eighty-five percent Mexican, eighty percent Puerto-Rican, fifty percent miscellaneous, twenty percent white men."

(I don't mention to Willie that his percentages don't exactly add up.)

"Den when you in dere, dey give you a bag lunch: a baloney sandwich three-inch thick, a cookie, cracker, 'n juice.

"Dey got workin' inmates will give you your clothes.

You put 'em on. Dey give you boxers, but dey don't give you no Fruit of the Loom. You go around the corner to see the doctor. A doctor takin' your blood pressure. You see the dentist, and the dick doctor. You had to grab your pee, and he take a Q-tip and he stick it up in there. Shit that hurt.

"Some of the guys didn't make it downstairs in time to get deir clothes, so some of 'em were naked when dey see the doctors.

"We go back to the bull pen, and dey tell you what division to go to. Dey sent me to the dorm where young kids go. I was nineteen, going on twenty, and I was scared like dey all scared, the new ones like me.

"Dey had rows a bunks with a TV and AC. The other prisoners ax who you ride with. You say who you ride with the Vise Lord, GD [Gangster Black Disciple], Gangsters, Soul, Snakes, Latin King. Den whatever gang you ride with, dey take you aside and screen you. If you not one of the gangs, you a neutron. It's a good thing too, to stand on your own. [To be a neutron.] See, you a man before anythin'. Even gangs, dey respect a man for standin' up for his self and a gang. If dey like you, dey take you under deir wing. If you lie, dey beat your ass.

"Each gang had a leader, a chief – he know all the laws. You have to pay your dues. Dey had a poor box – all the gangs. Dey point you to a guy. He get you soap, deodorant, tooth paste, pencil, paper, food. The gang give it to ya. Den if you don't have money, den when you get money, you buy somethin' and put it back inta the box.

"If someone steal, and dey get caught, dey might get hurt – get a finger broken.

"In prison you don't use that word: bitch. If you call someone a bitch and he don't do somethin' – don't stand up for his self and be a man – den rumor is gonna spread, and dey're gonna come after him.

"You get inta alotta fights. Some people get fightin' over the TV. Sometimes over other stuff. I tried to stay away from all dat shit. I just wanted to mind my own business, but I never let anyone mess with me even though I was scared. I didn't let 'em see dat.

"Dey used to give us jugs of Kool-aid from the kitchen. Everybody supposed to get a cup a Kool-aid. Whatever gang dat controlin' dat floor – the deck – go first and get as much as dey want. The neutrons go with the flow.

"People got alotta time on deir hands so dey did alotta gamblin' – poker or spades, mostly. Dey gamble with food from the commissary or off deir trays.

"Den you got guys dat lift weights all day. You got guys dat read all day. You got guys dat play cards all day. Dey all share the same toilet. Back in the day, when I was in dere, dey didn't have cameras. Now dey all got cameras.

"When you young, you're fightin' for respect. Everybody fought. A guy can look at you wrong, and you say a smart remark and dey say a smart remark back. You young, you wild, you naive. I didn't fight, but dey had gang fights in the kitchen or in the yard.

"Did eight months dere, back and forth to court. I took a bench trial. It's where you and a judge and your lawyer [public defender] and the state, work it out. You let one person decide your life verses a court.

"Dey found me guilty even though I changed my appearance. I started to wear a full beard. The man dat came to court; he didn't know who I was. My momma bought me a suit and paid fifteen hundred dollars for a lawyer.

"It took a good hour and a half. The judge said nobody know who I was. The police didn't even know who I was, and half of the charge wasn't right, so the judge threw dat out.

"He say, 'The reason I found you guilty, Mr. Triplett, is for the doctor bills dis man had to pay. I sentence you to three years in the state penitentiary.' Den he gave me a month's stay in the county jail (before going to the state jail).

"April 19 I turned twenty-one. I left at five o'clock in the mornin' on a Blue Bird bus – it wasn't blue – to Joliet Penitentiary. First I think I was in the West House. You locked down for twenty-four hours. Den you start seein' doctors and dentist… all the help.

"Dey had eight galleries, four on each side. Two people in a cell, fifty-two cells in a gallery. And every floor had a rail. Someone could be thrown off the rail if dey get into trouble. I never seen in happen, but I heard about it.

"After your twenty-four hours up, you had the opportunity to go out to the yard. Dey had twenty phones, ten on each side. You can walk, and dey had a basketball court and a gym. You walk from the gallery to the shower house. The shower house had eight poles with showers all around. You got booty bandits watchin' you so you don't drop the soap. If you drop the soap, don't ever pick it up. You get ten to fifteen minutes to take a shower. You go back to your cell. You do dis every other day. If in the population, [in the general population of all the inmates, not in solitary] you can shower every day.

"Den you go to the kitchen. Dey feed five hundred people. Once you go in the kitchen, you see the buck shot in the ceilin'. Dat was to stop the gangs from fightin'. There's alotta fightin' in the kitchen. Den you learn how to carry yourself like a wimp or a tough guy. If you think you're tough, dere's always a tougher guy.

"You have ta sit at the right table, at a Vise Lord table or a GD table. You know by the color of deir clothes which table is which. Mexican are Latin King and Puerto Ricans is Latin Disciples – depends on where you growed up at. Now a days, dey might be mixed up. The organization [gangs] changed. Now in prison dere's no respect of who dey talk to or how dey talk. It's all about a dollar. Everybody try and get a dollar sellin' drugs, sellin' anythin'.

"You come through the cafeteria line, you might have GD first or Latin King first. A Latin King or GD servin' you food, but he cool with dese other organizations. Dey have respect for you. You get in line. Dey served your food. Everyone loved the chicken. Dey served up all kind'a food.

You tell 'em what you want. Get your fork and spoon. You look and see where your crowd is. All the gangs have colors. GBD [Gangster Black Disciples] have blue, Vise Lord had gold and black... Everyone got deir own different color.

"Every man is scared in prison, and if dey say dey ain't scared, den dey lyin'. You scared, too. So you have to find out your image [what you project to others], so nobody can see dat you scared. I'm responsible for me. Every man is scared of another man if he ain't never been dere befo'– a curiosity fear."

Now I see where Willie gets some of his strut. It was part of his persona, his image in prison. He was pretty impressionable, turning twenty-one years old when he went in, and even though he had some street smarts, he still relied on his friends or his uncle to help him when he was in a tight spot. In prison he was on his own among a very rough crowd. Plus, it was a completely new environment. He didn't know the rules. He didn't know the routine. I'm sure he was afraid for his life. I know he was afraid about getting raped. I think I'd learn to strut, too.

"The inmates run everythin'. The state allowin' dem to have a job. If you don't have no skills, dey teach you dose skills, to keep you in line, to occupy your time. But some people just go to school, dey don't have no job.

"I'll tell you how it was in dere. The inmates, dey tell you what to do. The officer acts like he run the prison, but he don't. So you do what you have to do, follow the rules, the rules of the gangs, the rules of the prison, so you can get out. The biggest fear is not comin' home. When you in dere, you always dreamin' of comin' home.

"When you first go into the prison dey give you a number you'll never forget. Mine is N31268. Dat's the number. I don't care where I go around the world, dat's my number. Everyone has dat number, the FBI, CIA. Dat's the number you don't want 'em to know; it identifies you by your street life.

"Another thing about Joliet, you free to go to the law library. You have lots of intelligents [intelligent people in prison]. I don't think there is dumb human bein'. Dey learned a lot before dey got in prison. So just bein' a human bein', livin' on the street, dey know a lot.

"I stayed in Joliet for a month. Den dey shipped me off to Pontiac, Illinois prison. Dese are 100 percent killers in dere. Sometimes the most dangerous ones were the small guys. I was twenty-one when I went to Pontiac.

"The first day I was in dere I was walkin' on the first floor gallery, me and my celly. We walkin' to the cell. I'm closer to him den anybody dere even though we only know each other one day.

"Dis guy next to my cell, he said, 'Bitch, you owe me some money.'

"I didn't know if he was talkin' to me or my celly. I'm already scared. I had to put this tough imagine on; I ain't nobody's bitch. That's a code. Don't let no one call you a bitch. Dey had booty bandits here, too. Dey been dere years. Dey rape mens.

"He must of seen some fear. I did push-ups, but I was goin' to church.

"I say, 'You ain't talkin' to me you punch ass nigger.'

"He say, 'Yes I am. I'm gonna get the po-lice to unlock my cell and I'm gonna punch you.'

"Soon as the police come. Dey let him out. He had three locks on his door. First one at the end of gallery, den two locks on his cell door. He must have had it planned on how to get out.

"'Didn't I tell you I'm gonna beat your ass?'

"He told my celly to get the hell out. He push the bed in front of the door so I couldn't get out. I knew I had to fight or I was gonna be somebody's bitch.

"I wooped his ass so bad. He hollered. Everybody hear dis hollerin'– eight floors on each side. Everyone knows it's a fight. The officer tell me to stop beatin' him.

"He was a Gangster I found out.

"Whoever was runnin' the gallery came down [a prisoner].

"The officer had to let him out. The officer gave him a ticket. [The man Willie beat up.]

"Dis guy, he axed me, 'What you ride?'

"I didn't say nothin'.

"He said, 'If you weren't a church boy [a Christian], I'd come kick your ass.' See, church guys is an organization, too. He thought I was a church guy.

"He say to the other guy I beat up, he say, 'You know

the law. If he no faggot when he come in, you can't turn him to a faggot.'

"The officer let us out.

"You see someone do somethin', you see it, but you don't see it. You hear it, but you don't hear it. You don't tell. You never tell.

"Dey made the guy pay 'bout 50 cartons [of cigarettes. "Dey" is the gang that is running the gallery Willie is in.] Dis guy I beat up, he a man before anythin'. In order to keep things cool with the gangs, he had to pay the Vise Lords to avoid a war. He had to pay the poor box. Every group have a poor box. If you take somethin' from the poor box, later he gotta replace it.

Everyone gotta pay dues, too. You pay dues once a month: food, clothes, money. "Everyone got ta pay for protection, too. Dat's one of the codes.

"Now I get respect. Alotta respect!

"Respect mean a lot in dere. If you got called a name, you beat the man. Don't take shit from no one. Den if you don't do anythin', you were prime for rape. You the new bitch whether you liked it or not.

"I didn't tell nobody I was a Vise Lord.

"I see a guy I know. He a Vise Lord.

"He say, 'Why didn't you tell nobody you hooked up?'

"He showed me around, where my crowd is, to learn who to talk to, who to hang with. It's like in school. Once you get to know dem, dis is your crowd, dis is gonna be who you hang out with. I didn't want to get into any organizations, I just want to lay back and go to church, do the right thing.

"Just like at Joliet, you got alotta time on your hands. Some days we went to the gym, shot pool, played handball or cards, or get in a fight. You'd lose recreation time if you were fightin'. You'd do whatever to make the time go by.

"Sometimes dere was wars, gang wars. You can tell when it's gonna be a war, it's real quiet, You can hear a pin drop. Somethin' gonna go down, so you better keep your eyes open."

"Were you ever in a war?" I asked.

(I know Willie has a bit of a temper. He has gotten into trouble when he wasn't in prison because of it. I can easily see him getting into a fight in this type of environment, a good excuse to let off some understandable frustration due to the situation he was in.)

"I was in a war in the yard. I didn't get involved, I just seen it. Prob'bly somethin' about drugs or money. The guards call for help and the guys in the tower, dey shoot in the air and make us lay on the ground. Den you all go inside. We get locked down."

"The guards in the yard don't have guns?"

"No. Just the guys in the towers. If the guards in the yard have guns, dey might get taken, so dey just got walkie talkies."

Man, I think, *If I were a guard, I wouldn't want yard*

duty. But then probably none of the guards within the prison have guns, or even tasers (if they had tasers back then). Anything they carried could be taken and used against them.

I hope they pay those people well!

"I had to see more doctors when I went dere, to see if dere anythin' wrong with me. Dey find I had TB, 'cause I got bit.

(I don't explain to Willie you don't get TB from being bitten. It really doesn't matter, so I let it go.)

"Dey calculated fourteen months off my three years, for good time [for good behavior]. I got good behavior 'cause I went to school, and I worked in the kitchen. [That's good behavior.]

"When I was in dere, I heard about a woman dere dat got killed. She been workin' dere for like thirty years. She was a guard. She was screwin' dese gang leaders. One day dis guy tried to come on to her, and she said no, and he raped her and killed her.

"The gang she with, dey found out she got killed. I wasn't in the kitchen dat day.

"Dey made him tell on his self. The gang leader tell the guy dat did it, he has to tell on his self. You have to take your own weight. The gang will kill you if dey find out you did it and you don't say you did. Dey still killed 'im. If he go from one penitentiary to another penitentiary, dey still have a hit on him; word get around.

"When I first went to the penitentiary I was twenty-one, on my birthday.

"Dey got bars and four locks on every cell. The first

lock when the officer let the gate up. The second lock on the gallery. The third lock is the dead lock [on the cell door]. The fourth one is yourself."

Willie is in jail until 1983. He was in there a little less than a year. As he mentions, he gets out early for good behavior. Willie had a year and a half of parole left when he was released. Willie said parole in Illinois is different than in Wisconsin.

"In Illinois if you called the parole officer one time a month for three months, den you were good. Den all you have to do is six months, unless you get caught again."

When Willie gets out, he starts working at Nena Enterprise making frames for office furniture. He works there for about four years.

I ask him if he was drinking and drugging at this time. He said he wasn't, he was just "smokin' weed." Obviously, Willie doesn't consider weed, or marijuana, a drug, and I suppose when you've done the kind of drugs Willie has done, it really isn't much of one.

Willie gets fired from Nena after a Mexican employee runs over his foot with a pallet jack. He beats him up and gets fired.

Willie explains what happened in a letter he sent me while in prison.

The reason I got into the fight was he was

tryin to show of[f] to a sexy Mexican hoe (whore), and he ran my toes over with a pallet jack. He start to babble in Spanish to the girl and began to laugh at me! The Mexican girl just gave him a funny look, like that shit wasn't funny. I told him fuck with me again and I'll kick your mother fucking ass. So he did it again. I beat his bitch ass.

I beat him so bad, I knocked him to the ground and jumped on top of him, beating his funky ass face in. Next thing I know he was snitchin to the supervisor and I was fired on the spot! After that I got the job at Predential Faldeo. I was there for 3 years. I was partying and going to the roller disco partys.

Chapter 6

Willie's First Introduction to Cocaine

~~~~~~~~

This is a letter that someone transcribed for Willie while he was in jail in Wisconsin. I received many letters from Willie while he was incarcerated. He wrote a few of them himself, but for the most part, Willie dictated his letters to someone else. I think writing was too much work for him. I'm sure he just sweet-talked someone else into doing it for him. There was little punctuation or capitalization in this letter, so, for easier reading, I have added those things. The exclamation points are all Willie's, however. Otherwise the letter is unchanged. Be forewarned; this is a bit graphic.

I remember all this happing in March of 1988, when I first started freebasing cocain witch was new being called crack cocain. It was a hot sunny day. I was working at a factory called predentual Faldco. Oh and before I forget, this is the second part of the fist letter I wrote to you. When me and Lina first started getting high, my perception of the world was much different. The world was a crazy place. I had always tried to be a gentleman, but I was also relizing that women didn't always prefer a gentlemen. When I took that first hit with Lina, I relized I had a deep dark side to me. When I started gettin' high, I would have wild freaky sex doing all kinds of dirty things like eatin' the pussy. To me coain was a freaky love drug. I would blow the smoke all over her naked body.

When I was a kid, my uncle told me to never eat pussy, it was no good. Only white boys ate pussy. Once Lina took a hit, held it in and began suckin' my dick, she made me feel amazing. That was the first time she swallowed my cum. I began to love having sex along with getting high!

Lina was a fine bitch in her day. She told me to take a huge hit and hold it in as long as possible and I got unbelievably high. I was a complete sexual freak. She began to suck, lick, and touch all over my body. I never relized how many *people had a dark side. Once she brought a dildo and I played with her the whole time we got high. After we got high, Lina left to go home. I didn't see her again for 2 months. The next time I saw her it was almost my birthday. She came over with one of her girl friends. They brought a $50 sack of powder cocain and we free based it. We had a freaky 3 some. I was eating so much pussy, my jaw was soar. At that time I didn't think I was an addict. I thought I was just havin' fun.*

I began spending all of my money. My bank account went dry! I was living in a 3 story building when all this was going on. My uncle helped me find the place. He used to live there. My land lords name was Edna Sunshine Price; a fine ass black woman.

When I first moved there, I was about 25 years old. Bein a young man, I always like the older women at that time. I was hittin' on Edna and she said I'm old enough to be your mama. I'm 65 year old. She said I don't have any kids. I would like you to be my son! Then we became like mother and son. She would let me drive her beat down station wagon sometimes. She called the wagon Ol Betsie. IT had a large hole in the floor. I helped her out around the house whenever I could. I loved her like a mother and I still do today, even tho she's dead and gone. I'll never forgot the words she said on her death bed – "Son, keep doin what your doin". I met her boyfriend Cardnal, an African barbodian native. He did construction. At this time I was only smokin' pot. Oh sorry. This is before I was using cocain. She knew I smoked weed and didn't care. She called it "funny cigarettes".

Back to Lina. I had my B-day with Lina and Betty. I constantly had the urge to get high. After Ms. Price died, I had a nervous breakdown. She helped me be a responsible young man. Witout her, I felt lost. I began to lose a lot of tings because of my getting high! The fucked up part was I didn't care. I had lost everything I worked so hard to get. I just wanted to get high! I worked with a family by the name of Hoose. They introduced me to a guy named David. I helped David get an apartment in Ms Price's building. I didn't know at the time David was a heavy drug user. Ms. Price thought that David was a pussy, but she let him move in 2 days later on the second floor.

A few Buddys came by and we went downtown to smoke weed and chase girls. I was the odd guy in the group. Everyone but me had earrings in their ears. Mama or Ms. Price told me I should get my ears pierced. Me and David went and got our ears pierced. I payed for him and told him to pay me back when he got payed. The on(e) day in April,

David came and asked me if I wanted to get high. I didn't like gettin' high with a guy, so I left to find me a girl. I asked David to leave. I went and got $200 out of the bank and got high with a neibor hood girl.

At one point in our friendship, me and David had a falling out. I had borrowed him $50 and he didn't make it a priority to pay me back. After Ms. Price had died, I was responsible for collection the rent, and David decided to stop paying his rent. After I would collect the rent, I would give it to Ms. Price's sister, Mary. Before Ms. Price, I had saved $2800.00, and I had Mr. P. hold onto it.

CHAPTER 7

WILLIE'S TRIP TO MADISON

~~~~~~~

I pick Willie up at his home on the east side, and he says he has a restaurant he likes that he wants to go to for lunch. In the typical Willie style, he doesn't tell me the name of the place or where it is, he just gives me directions on how to get there. My guess is he doesn't know the name or he doesn't know how to pronounce it. It is a Spanish restaurant with a Spanish name.

After we finish our meal, I ask the waitress if it's okay if we sit for a while. It's not a problem, so we begin.

"Thank you too for lunch, baby," he says to me.
I let the "baby" slip by.
"You're welcome, Willie."

"Do your husband ever tell you you's a fine mother fucker?"

"He doesn't say words like that, Willie. Not to me."

"What he supposed to say?"

"That's not polite. Not for white people, anyway." (I laugh).

"Okay."

I can see Willie puts this away for the future use.

"Let's talk about how you came to Madison."

"Well, it was a Saturday around two o'clock in the evenin'. It was a sunny day. I was standin' on the corner and somebody gave me two dollars. And Popeye Chicken had dis special, two pieces of chicken and a biscuit – dere weren't no fries with dat. And I go to Popeye's and order me some food. I see dis man sittin' at the table with his wife and his family. I go over deir and I ax him, can he buy me a soda. He tell me, 'No.'

"Bein' the smart ass I was, still a no-good-guy who drinkin' and druggin', I said, 'If I was robbin' you, you'd be glad to give me your money.' Den I walked over to the table.

"Now he come back 'bout five minutes. He said God tol' him to buy me a soda. Now I'm sayin' in my own mind, he's given me dis God crap.

"So I say, 'Okay, buy me a soda.'

"We got to talkin' and he ax me have I been saved. I say, 'Ya, I been saved, I been baptized and all dat.'

"Before I got dose two dollars, I went to West Street

behind dis fancy restaurant in deir dumpster and took a steak outta dere. Somebody done ate off the steak and a baked potato. It was still wrapped up in dat foil, and I took it and put it in my buggy."

"In your buggy?"

"Yeah, like a shoppin' cart.

"In my buggy I had a blanket, and a barbeque grill. At dat time I was goin' into Jewels' garbage can (a grocery store). I take the food out, raw food, 'cause the date had expired. I was cookin' it on the grill."

"You had a grill?" (Insert an amazed look here.)

"You know one of dose small grills you take off somebody's porch. Outside the store dey have the coals. Den you go inside the store and you take some lighter fluid, and you go outside where you camp at night and cook it, if you ain't high already or chasin' girls. Dat's what you did in Chicago back in dem days."

"So you had all this stuff in your buggy?"

"Dat was before I met the guy. We ate Popeye Chicken, and he was preachin' to me about God and all dis. I'm drinkin' and druggin'. I wanna get high, not listen to dis guy preachin'. I must'a been on a run, a drug run. I was hangin' out in the street for like four or five days, and I was tired. So I stayed at dat corner to get me somethin' to eat.

"So the guy say, 'Where is your family?'

"I say, 'I don't know where my family is.' He was bein' nosy. He might have been interested in me, but I ain't sure.

"He say, 'If you had a chance, would you leave Chicago?'

"I say, 'Sure, I'd leave Chicago!'

"He say, 'What about your family?'

"I say, 'I ain't got no family. I'd leave right now.'

"So the guy say, 'Okay.' He say, 'First I got to go to Kim and Baker; dey be church people and dey be havin' a seminar.

"So we went to dis church seminar. Dey was preachin' God. And dey start askin' for some money. I say, 'I ain't got no money.' So after the seminar, we drive to Madison."

"What year was this?"

"Probably in 1999. So I was homeless for fifteen to twenty years before I came to Madison. I could've went home, but I was too independent for me.

"We got in his truck and came to Madison. I ain't never heard of Madison, Wisconsin. I heard of Milwaukee, Wisconsin because I been dere once. I didn't like Milwaukee because dey too racist.

"He put me in a hotel, the Red Hotel. Dey went home. I looked at myself in the mirror. Seemed like I weighted eighty pounds. Dat's how thin and skinny I was. I was smokin' alotta dope at dat time. You don't eat, and when you gettin' high all day, you lose alotta weight.

"Dat was the first beginnin' of my life change when I left Chicago. When I left dat Popeye Chicken and came to Madison, dat when my life begin, bein' a human bein' all over again.

"I got in the hotel dat night. I took a shower. I was glad to get in the bed. I didn't know what a bed was 'cause I done slept on the ground anywhere in Chicago. Dat Sunday mornin' he came and picked me up. His wife give me some leftover rice and chicken. Dey took me to a church, a school place. About five o'clock dat evenin' he took me to the shelter. He said he come to get me the next day to show me around in Madison. He gonna show me around, where to get a job and dis and dat.

"So I say, 'Okay.'

"Monday came. I still at the hotel. He said he gonna call me at nine o'clock, but he done never get dere. I get upset for a little while. So I tried to call him. No answer. About three o'clock later on dat day, I get in touch with his wife.

"She say, 'You go to the temp service and get a job?'

"I say to myself, I don't' know my way around. I say, 'Where's your husband?'

"She say, 'He's at work.'

"I say, 'Okay.'

"Den she say, 'We'll definitely come and get you tomorrow.'

"Den when Tuesday came, dey didn't show up again, so I called dem. Dey didn't never answer the phone. Now my street knowledge kick back in. I start walkin' around myself to see what's goin' on, what kind'a territory I'm in, what kind'a neighborhood. The shelter have dis thing dat you have to be at the shelter all day. In Chicago it ain't like dat. Chicago have alotta different drop in centers around dere where you can sit around all day.

"Wisconsin have one, but it too far away, and people didn't tell me about it.

"Later on dat night we get in line at six thirty, and dey let us in at eight o'clock. I meet a staff named Frank. Nice guy. He was a recoverin' her-o-in addict.

"I say, 'Where's the work service around here?'

"He say, 'Midwest is on East Washington and Hancock.'

"So I get up. I went to Midwest Labor. Dey tell me to fill out an application. So I filled out an application, and dey didn't give me no work.

"Dey say, 'Come back the next day.'

"So I went back the next day. And dey still didn't send me out. Dey sent me out the next day to get a job. Dey was payin' me three dollar an hour or maybe less. Dat give me a little pocket money. About twenty dollars, maybe less.

"So I ask Frank again, 'Where the other temp service I hear about call Labor Ready?'

"He say, 'Labor Ready's farther down, but you have to be dere early, really early.'

"So what I did the next day, I got up at three o'clock in

the mornin', and I walked to Labor Ready. It was 'bout an hour walk, but I was hustlin'. The place open at five. So as I got dere, I filled out an application. I was the first guy in line. It was first come, first serve. Dey played it dat way. Dey gave me a job. So I went out and made me some money. I almost made about twenty dollars.

"I started to go to Labor Ready every day. I got to know dat staff, the womens dere. I got to know one of the bosses, Tim. So as I got to know dem, dey see I was determined to work, so dey made sure I had a steady ticket. Dat's when I met Mary, Hanna, Tim, Shirley. Dems the five peoples I met. And Sally. Den I met dis guy named Tommy. He called himself a player, but he wasn't a player, but he had the girls. He had two nice cars. Lean. Nice wheels. Dey sent me and Tommy on a ticket together. Tommy was tryin' to hit on Hanna. So we started partyin' together after we get outta work, and Hanna was one of the supervisor girls. She made sure we had tickets every day.

"So for a year and a half, I started savin' money up."

"A ticket is a job?"

"Dey give you a ticket, and you go out to a job site.

"Me and Tommy got tickets regular 'cause he liked Hanna and Hanna liked him. Everyone at the office was friends, and next thing you know we all start hangin' out. Tommy had the car and the girl. Mary had a car. All dem had a car except me.

"We started going to bars, but I wasn't doin' drugs. I had made a substitute to smokin' weed and drinkin'."

"How did you do that? How did you substitute smoking weed and drinking for cocaine? I would think that would be hard to do."

"I didn't wanna go back. I wanted ta change. I didn't wanna spend all my money on dat, so I made the substitute.

"I did dat for a year and a half, and I saved up alotta money to get me an apartment. Den I bought me a little car. A '84 Cadillac Sedan. I bought it from my roommate Mark when he died.

"I found out Madison had alotta gays and lesbians here. My roommate, he was a gay guy. He ain't never been around a black man in his life, dis close.

"One day I was shinin' my shoes, and he say, 'Blacks really shine deir shoes for real?' 'Cause he been in the army, and he heard alotta jokes about it.

"I say, 'Yeah, I really shine my shoes.'

"'You all dress the way dey say you-all dress, but you-all different.'"

"I sat, 'We ain't no different then you-all.'"

"So me and Mark became friends."

"Mark is your roommate?"

"Mark was my landlord. He was gay. But he was a strong alcoholic. He drank a fifth a gallon of vodka every day, all night. Once he told me to take my rent money, two hundred dollars, to buy him some liquor with it. I was makin' like thirty dollars a day, and dat was good. I was puttin' my rent money on the side. Sometimes I went and bought two gallons of vodka and dat was it for the rent.

"While I was livin' dere, with Mark, I met Dis Indian girl named Billy. She was a dumb bitch. She was datin' me, and she was in love with another guy. But I didn't care. I just said, 'Give me some.'

"One day we was in bed havin' sex, and she came right out and say she in love with another guy.

"I say, 'So. It don't bother me.'

"Dat cut my bridge off again in a relationship. So here I am, tryin' to do the right thing and it didn't work."

This is a big clue to Willie's Achilles' heel, or at least one of them.

CHAPTER 8
Willie's Heel

I drive over to the halfway house Willie is living in on the east side of town to get more material down for his book. He has repeatedly told me via phone messages or during previous discussions that he wants to talk about love. I finally I relent. I have put off this discussion because I'm thinking this is just going to be mostly Willie philosophizing. The man does like to talk. It ends up being that way, in part, but only because this is an important topic to Willie on a few different levels and one he has spent many an hour running through his mind. I'm not sure he can speak for all addicts, but it is obvious to me he is speaking about himself.

"When a person who have an addict problem, we always

lookin' for love in the wrong places because deep inside we lonely, and we want someone to love us. Even though people tell us dey love us, we still not sure a dat. We put a force field of a rejection around us. It's like instant gratification. I want my love right dere, when I want it. Right now.

"But it ain't dat way because we really don't know how to love. We tell a person we love 'em. We may say dat, but deep inside we don't because we don't really know how to love ourselves. See what I'm sayin'?

"As a child, your mom and dad tell you, I love you, I love you, dis and dat. You wanna find out what it is. See, dey showin' a different kind of love.

"But den when you get a certain age, when you start noticin' your feelin's, you start gettin' crazy different feelin's and different thoughts.

"Well, I need to find me a girl or whatever your choice preference may be. You want someone to come and nurture your flush [flesh]. Your flush is your so-called love, but it ain't love. Alotta people tell you in dier heart dats true love, but true love to me is dat you don't have to tell nobody you love 'em, you just show it.

"Because people got dis word, constantly throwin' around the word, dey say, 'I love you, I love you, I love you.' But deep inside you want your flush to be happy. Your flush wanna be loved by another flush.

"The flush is never happy at all. It ain't never happy. You got dis feelin' inside of your flush dat what you got, it can't prob'bly be true love, and it start turnin' you upside down, and you wonderin' what makin' dis happen. Where is dat love at?

"You grow older. You think about the love your parents give you. Den you start gettin' the love from your parents. Den you wanna share it with another human bein'. The other human bein' ain't gonna automatically give you the same love dat you say you want. Dat what make you as a human bein' go out and say, 'I gotta find somethin' different to make me happy.'"

"Is that drugs?"

"Right. You already know what make you happy. But your flush ain't happy, 'cause your flush can't do the thing dat it wanna do. It might be a wild thing or a crazy thing or a thing you seen in your past or you seen on TV, and you wanna explore and get to likin' it, and it look good. So you go out dere and see if you can find it."

"Like what you had with Lina."

"Yeah, like what I had with Lina.
"And den you find out dat ain't love. Den you go right back to the drawin' board. What is dat love?
"But dis flush ain't never satisfied. Some people say, I love my dog. You can see dat kind'a love. The dog showin' his love all the time. Every time you walkin' down the street he waggin' his tail. He wanna lick you, kiss you. He's showin' his appreciation. We as humans, we have an addic-

tion of tellin' people, I love you, I love you. Den we look at the other person straight in the eye den we lie to 'em. Den we turn around and go somewhere else.

"When I was out dere drinkin' and druggin', I was in love with drinkin' and druggin'. I wasn't in love with no women. I wasn't in love with nobody. It made my soul peaceful, but I can't find the true love. But my flush found the wrong love all the time because it was satisfied by drinkin,' it was satisfied with drugs, whatever made it feel good. The flush was satisfied.

"Deep down you still ain't found the true love. You sit dere and wonder and dis and dat. Whatever higher power dey called God, when he told Adam dat he gonna make a women outta him and he say, okay. Den he turn around and say, she's made of my flush and bone. The flush already a man, den he learned dat dat was love. Because dat was created, it came from his thought. It came out to be a livin' soul. Den it just like a human bein'. Den you come out together and you know your flush like to be loved to another flush. Just like your spirit, it wanna be loved by another spirit. Everythin' wanna be loved by the same.

"Just like birds of a feather flock together. Dey lovin,' dey flyin' around, hangin' out. Same as a drug addict, alcoholic, you love hangin' out with dem type of people. But deep inside, you ain't found love. Your flush is love because dat will make you feel good, but deep inside, your soul know it ain't happy."

Willie Lee Triplett

At this point I can tell it really hurts Willie that he hasn't found the love that he is looking for, this true love as he describes it. And I don't think it's just about the sex; sex is important to Willie, of course – it's tightly mixed up in his addictions – but I think Willie is as insecure as the rest of us. I think besides companionship, Willie feels he will have more self-worth, feel more whole when he has someone who loves him.

When you've been there already, already had someone other than a family member love you, you know that is not the case. But you see, Willie has never had this type of love, even as a young man. He's never been head-over-heels in love with someone and had them head-over-heels in love with him back. I feel sorry for him. As painful as that first love can be sometimes, it's something I think everyone should experience, at least once in their life.

Then Willie's conversation about love takes a different turn.

"In order for your soul to be happy, your soul always lookin' for the true love. The true love is the Creator, whoever you call your God. Who I call my God, dat is the love. It always peaceful, it always warm. But every time you turn around bein' a human bein', your flush see somethin' different, and it want a part of it. Everybody want somethin'.

"When I was out on the streets, alotta guys dey was married. And still today, dey might have a great wife at home, but what dey see in deir flush, dey want another woman, even though dey know dey got a wife at home. It's the same for a woman. She might control herself a little bit, but she see a guy and her flush tell her, I wanna try. But deep inside, her spirit tell her it's wrong. Her flush tell her: Dis how I like to be love, dis how I liked to be hold, dis how I like to be comfort. Just like the TV tell you, an armored knight gonna save you. But dey lyin'. An armored knight is like the flush. The flush ain't gonna be true. Sooner or later, we as human bein's, we ax, what is true love?

I think Willie has figured out a thing or two.

"Now if you married, or whatever, your flush just hangin' out, just seein' other flush walk around every day. Or your flush might see her flush do somethin' to turn him on, and his flush like it, and so he say, 'I love dat flush.'

"You see, nothin' gonna last forever. We tell ourselves, it's gonna last forever. But den one partner or another say, 'I can't make dis person happy.' I'm tryin' to make dis person happy, but it just ain't workin'. When you stop doin' what you doin' when you first met, dat love vanish. He ain't gotta do dat stuff no more. He got it already, his love. So he go outside and explore and find love somewhere else. Den you sit dere and you wonder why dis ain't happenin'.

"Den your spirit try to keep the flush in control. So it won't go out the comfort zone, so it keep holdin' on, to learn how to love.

"But we are people. We have so many different things

in the world change our thinkin' constantly. Back in the days, dey didn't have dat many change in thinkin' of love. Dey didn't know love, but dey found what love was.

"Like in 1914, dey had respect, dey had better morals den today. I ain't sayin' dat love is not dere, all I'm sayin' is today our flush has too many toys to attract it. Dey might had alotta toys den too, but dey had everythin' more secret, and dey stuck with deir family and everythin' for love. Den the flush startin' to learn how to love the spirit together."

"What made you think of all this stuff? I mean you've been in relationships before. I know you've told me a couple things about them. Sometimes drugs messed it up, and sometimes other things messed it up."

"You know what made me think about it is dat sometimes I want somebody to just go to the movies and hang out. I want to go take somebody to dinner just to show my appreciation, so I can show some love to somebody. But love ain't never come back. But when I did try and find love, back den I was drinkin' and druggin' hard.

"Now since I got in the program, I wanna learn how to do a new love. Call somebody up or see if I can take 'em to dinner or to a movie or somethin'.

"But you can't find no nice girls. I ain't sayin' dere ain't no nice girls out dere. Just same as for the girls, dey say dey can't find no nice guys out dere. Den you got mens and womens takin' whatever dey can sell to make deir flush happy.

"I'm gonna talk about different cultures now, of love. See black womens, dey have mens, but dey don't have certain kind'a mens to choose from, like workin' mens goin' to a job. Dey have very few of dem. But alotta black womens have alotta drug dealer guys with nice cars. The womens wanna be comfort, wanna be happy, and dey wanna learn to share. Dey want a family. Dey want someone to buy dem a house, a home. See, deir body is deir house, and the drug dealers love the womens as dey are."

Willie is talking about prostitutes here. That is the majority of the black women Willie has known at the age of forty-nine.

"But dey know dese guys out dere, and dey know dey gonna cheat on 'em. Dat 'cause of the environment dat dey in, dealin', sellin' drugs, and deir behavior. Deir ain't a drug dealer dat I haven't met haven't cheated on his woman. Dey have the night girl out dere to get with dem, or dey get another girl dat dey know in the neighborhood, and dey take her. Dey don't have no respect for her.

"In my days, back in the 70s, black women have a little few to choose from – the workin' men. Now alotta young black mens don't wanna take time into gettin' a job, doin' a job. I ain't sayin' dey don't wanna work. I'm sayin' dey see so much of dat fast money, quick money, nice cars, dat somebody work all deir life for, and dey already got it. Den come along a black women and she see dis and want dem to take her to a movie. Dey know nine outta ten dey want the guy to treat 'em right, but the guy ain't gonna treat 'em right. So dey go along with 'em because dey like the guy. Den once dey get to like 'em a little more, den dey start sayin' I love you. Den the black guy go along with the program, say the same thing. Dat's the behavior in drinkin' and druggin' and sellin' drugs. I know about two cultures pretty good.

"White men, when dey find a nice white girl, dey marry her real quick and have babies so nobody else can marry her. Dey get all what dey need with dat woman. Den dey get tired of her, and dey leave her. Dat what we call dey disin' her. She ain't no more use. Now the guy wanna go out dere. He wanna different taste of pie 'cause she ain't doin' like she was. So he wanna explore for his self what's out dere.

"Now dis nice girl, she was livin' so nice, now she wanna go find somethin' different 'cause her man done run out. Now she wanna find another man to replace dis one. But he done ruined her, hurt her feelin's. Dey both can do dat to each other.

"But white mens always get dese nice girls through the family or friend or the school. And dey take her home to momma and daddy. Den dey offer a marriage to dis girl quick, and she don't really know nothin' 'bout it. But he put her in a situation in front of her parents, so it's harder to say no because he said he love her. He might do, but he love the flush more den he love in his heart. He might at dat second.

He's tryin' to get the spirit to love his flush, same as the women. Den dey run away, and dey have kids for a while, and dey ain't happy no more.

"Black mans, dis how dey do it. Dey ain't gonna marry the girl at all. Dey just gonna be with her. Some of dem wanna get married but not many. Most of the black womens, dey wanna get married, dey wanna have a man, a family. The white men, dey marry des white womens fast before somebody else can. And dey be nice girls.

"I met some married mans who had a fine lookin' wife. And I say, 'Why you want another girl? He say, 'Man she don't do what she used to do.'

"See dats where the problem come in. You tell a person what you want, 'cause in a relationship, when you first meet a girl, a girl gonna tell you what she want, but she ain't gonna tell you quick. She wanna hear what you got to say first. Dat's a girl. Den when dey get a little more comfortable, she gonna start tellin' you her thoughts, her feelin's. Den she wanna see if he really interested. She gonna play a little shotgun game. Dat just a girl.

"Den the guy come along, and he go along with it. Den when a man and women start havin' sex, when dey just meet, it's enjoyment to both of dem. Deir flush be happy now, the flush came together, and what dey did, dey found out what dey like in each other, it's sex and other little feelin' dat come along with it. Dey lay in bed and cuddle. But deep inside somebody got a little doubt in deir mind. Dey ain't gonna tell one another dey got a little doubt because dey wanna make sure is dis true love or not. Den dey keep havin' sex. Den dey get into a point in life, dey say, 'Dis guys so nice to me, I think I love 'im.' She say dat to herself. And he say the same thing.

"And you start ta tell your buddies, and she start to tell her buddies. Dat's where the comfort come in. The guys say, 'I think I'm in love with dis girl.' But all dis time you lovin' the flush, even though you love the hangin' out part. Don't get me wrong. But den if you still sayin' you in love with dis individual, you gotta go back to the first drawin' board to keep doin' what you do to keep her. Dat the same as her, she got to do dat, too.

"When you first meet an individual, you gotta keep on doin' what you doin'. Before you do have sex, you gotta tell a person what you like so dey can make you happy, feelin' dat love. Dats what it is. Because if you never tell a person what you like doin', what you love, what make you feel good, den when you get married, be with 'em so long, it stop. He don't do dat no more. She don't do dat no more. You only a human bein'. Ain't nothin' you haven't done, haven't been done already. You beatin' around the bush just like him, goin' out, tryin' to satisfy your flush. Your flush lookin' for love."

"So do you do that when you're in relationship? Can you stay with one person?"

"I hided my feelin' from womens because of when I got hurt. Still today I don't trust no womens. In my mind it's like, I ain't met no good girl. I know dey out dere. From my point of view, bein' drinkin' and druggin' all my life, I always ran into people dat usin' me, and I usin' dem. I might'a, though I was in love, but I wasn't. I was was in love with drugs, in love with money. What made me feel dat I was in love? You did somethin' with me right dere in the moment.

"Say I met you right now and I say, 'let's do dis,' and you did it. Dat what make me fall in love. Dat's what I learned to like, because you didn't hide somethin' from me at dat moment. You weren't ashamed. You show love right dere on the spot. You don't say maybe next week and dis and dat. No. You show love right dere on the spot. Dat's love.

"Den me, when I got hurt a couple time, I broke it off because my mind got set dat ain't no good womens out dere. Dat changed about three weeks ago, dis year.

"How it changed? I did dis job. I see dis nice-lookin' lady, she had a nice figure and nice kid, dis and dat. She had a man. And I tried to figure it out; how do dey keep deir life goin'? She was nice to me. I think dere might be some nice womens out dere. So when I looked at it, she wasn't a young woman. She was about in her forties."

"Is this a black women or white?"

"She is a white woman. Dere is some black womens out dere, but dey don't really have my taste. Dat ain't sayin' dey ain't fine, dey into the fast boys, fast cars, dats what dey feel comfortable with. Den when you come into another environment like Madison, it's mostly street black womens. And if you catch a nice black women, she datin' a white boy. Dat's a problem to me in my eyesight.

"To my eyesight it's racsim. But the way I look at it, she doin' it for comfort. She know he got a little somethin' goin' on, know he got a house and dis and dat. His mom and dad gonna help. A black man get the leftover white womens from the white men, the ones dat were abused by the white men. Or dey just might like a black man, but dey ain't never dated a white man. Dats the eyesight I see.

"Just like Hollywood. Dey always showin' fine black womens with white mens. Some black mens don't like dat. Hollywood really don't show fine womens datin' black mens. We know it's out dere. If dey did show it, den the society always got somethin' to say about it. Den dey cut it out of the movie.

"Dis what the white man always say, 'You shouldn't be datin' a guy like dat. You should be datin' a white guy who got all dis goin', to Harvard' and dis and dat.

"Dat still ain't true love dat she lookin' for. But daddy brainwash her and momma brainwash her and say she should do dat. Den the little girl can't never grow up on her own. Find out her feelin's for herself. If she do find out the feelin's, daddy don't want to accept it.

"Black men don't wanna accept it, but dey live with it because it be forced on dem so many years in slavery to deal with dat love.

"Lena Horn said white men look at black women as fast and hoes. Dey got a fine fast body, and dey find some white womens fine, too. But deep inside we all still missin' dat love. Anything we see, we want somethin' different. Den I start to cover love up like I did. When I got into a bad relationship, I just hid my love from someone. I don't wanna be bothered with nobody. I just turn myself off. I don't care if she want me or not. I can get a night girl and get a piece a pie from her. I ain't gotta love her. But even though I can love her in a different way, I ain't gotta tell her dat. So dat solve dat problem. If I tell a night girl I love her, she know I'm lyin' because I'm payin' for it, and she'll go along with it.

"Dat's why I had an incident like dat last week. I went to Outback Steakhouse. I went with my friends, Dave and Bill. We had dis waitress. I tell her, I like to flirt, I like to talk crap. Dave said, 'Won't you ax her out?' I say, 'From my street knowledge, nine to ten she got a boyfriend.' Den she gonna give me some lame excuse, say she can't go out, or she doin' dis and dat. Dat's a game.

"Bill say, 'She got a ring on her finger.' Dat's what I told you, what white boys do all the time. A nice lookin' white girl, dey marry dem quick so nobody else can marry dem. Den dey get 'em pregnant. The girl say she love him, and the white boy say he love her, too. Boom. White girls always wait for dat boy to say I love you. Girls say dey love you, too, but white girls wait on deir boy to say I love you. Dis is from my experience. I know dem two different cultures.

"Den he say, 'Ax her.' So I axed her – dis show you what the girl thinkin' – she say, 'You gotta keep comin' to the Outback, den I think about it.' Dis tellin' me, I gotta keep spendin' sa'more money. I gotta keep payin' you five to ten dollar tip to see if you go out, but den you might not go out because you hustlin' me. Dey didn't understand dat. Dey say, 'She gave you a time and date of when she's workin' dere.' Dat still a game. I bet she got a boyfriend. 'Oh yeah. I got a boyfriend.' She started to give me all dese excuses, so I turned off. You ain't gotta lie to me 'cause I already know what's goin' on. Dat's why I turn myself off on women. I don't' wanna hear your lies.

"If I say I just wanna go hang out, let's just hang out. If I wanna piece a pie, let's just go and do it. Some people want to fight and chase 'em and dis and dat. No. I don't wanna do dat, 'cause I ain't used to dat. I don't think it's right. I don't feel it's right no more because I been hurt. How I look at it, I don't need it. A night girl give me a piece a pie, and she tell me she love me or she like me. And I can go on with dat big lie, at least I know she's lyin' to me. Dat's the way it is."

"But you still want to meet girls?"

"I still want dat.

"A big problem with dat is dat addiction part, the addiction and the rejection.

"You know when you out dere in the streets bein' homeless, people show you love. Dey show you love right dere on the spot. Dat's love and flush love. The soul and flush together. Dey showin' you dis kind'a love. When you in your addiction, you don't really believe people out dere love you. When I out dere sleepin' on the ground, people loved me. Dey brought me some food, dey took time outta deir schedule to help me, gave me clothes. Dat's love. Dey didn't see no smoke screens, no nothin' attached. And dey showin' deir flush love and deir spirit love. Dat's connected love of a human bein'.

"Like a man took me in one day named Reverend Dale. I was on 95th and Ashley. It was on a Saturday. I was out dere gettin' high all day long. I walked up to a man. I ax him, 'Can you give me a job?' He didn't hesitate. He say, 'Yeah, I give you job.' He was doing construction work. Dat was love. Dat was spiritual love and flush love. He took me in his house dat same day. He don't even know me. Dat's love. But still I didn't know what love was. I didn't know what comfort was. He gave me a place to stay in his own basement, den about four or five years later I end up robbin' the guy. His name was Reverend Dale. He was like a dad to me. He taught me carpenter work. He taught me all dese skills and everythin'. And right today I still use 'em. But dat's love, doin somethin' right dere on the spot. Ain't no embarrass, ain't no nothin'. Dat's the same, whoever your higher power might be.

"Same as Peter in the Bible. He call 'im over dere. God call 'im over, and at dat moment Peter had love. He walked on water. He didn't hesitate, he didn't do nothin'. So he start thinkin' dat love vanish. He start thinkin' about the flush dat was gonna drowned. Same as the man on the cross. Jesus, he thought about love, he thought about savin' his own life. Because Jesus kept preachin' about love, Jesus say, 'Take me.' Dat's love. When you do somethin' right dere on the spot. No hesitation. Just do it. You sharin' yourself.

"But we are people. We always take our eyes off love. Same as a person homeless. Dey don't think nobody love dem. Dey really don't. Because people don't show deir love with deir flush. Den when a person do give you somethin' when you homeless, dey showin' two love, one flush love and one spiritual love combined into one. Dey care about you as a person. Dey don't mind helpin'. Dey didn't hesitate. And you wonder, what's goin' on? And you know what's goin' on. Dey take deir time for you in deir busy schedule. Dat's love."

"But that's the easy part of love. The hard part is when you want a relationship and you don't trust anybody and you still want that. So what do you do about that?"

"You try and learn to change it. For somebody like myself, it's gonna take a long time. First of all, I don't wanna hear the rejection. I don't because I been drinkin' and druggin' so long dat I feel in my life, if you don't do somethin' right on the spot, you ain't showin' me no love. It ain't dat I want respect.

"First of all, everybody do somethin' on the first date. Some girls say, 'I don't do somethin' on the first date.' You done it because you already thought about it. See what I'm sayin'? But you still wanna put dis game of dis is love. Dey say patience is a virtue. Yeah, patience is good, but sometimes you gonna lose waitin' on somebody.

"Yeah, I might wanna nice young lady to go out, but she gotta be crazier den me. Dey have to wilder den me to know what I like. But right now, at dis moment, right now I don't care, 'cause I know somebody out dere tonight gonna solve my feelin' of dat love. Give me a piece a pie, and I can go about my business. I know I might fall in love with her how she made me feel. And it'd be good, 'cause I'm gonna deal with it, because she gonna bring me back, 'cause she done made me feel good."

"That's not the kind of love that lasts, though."

"But dat might be the good love dat I'm lookin' for. I really don't know a long-term love."

"But you were with someone in Champagne, Illinois, for how long?"

"You talkin' about Mary. I was with her for three years, but she didn't love me. She use'ded me, and I use'ded her. How I know dat? I was in the halfway house. The head of security, the ladies name was Debbie. And Debbie told the girl she don't love me. Dis is how I found out she didn't love me. I liked her. She made me feel good. I fell for her a little bit. But I didn't never tell her I love her.

"When I first met Mary I was goin' to work at County

Market, and I see her outside cryin'. She had a little boy named Davey. She started tellin' me her problems. I took advantage of dat, tryin' to get with her. But it didn't work. About a month went by and I see her. I just bought some Brut or Old Spice cologne.

"I say, 'I seen you before.'

"'No you didn't.'

"'Oh yes I did, at the bus stop with your son Davey.'

"And she say, 'Yeah.' Den she start remember right.

"She say, 'Do you need a ride.'"

"And I say, 'No.'

"'Can I meet you later on?'

"'Sure. I have to go to dis drug program tonight.' I tell her I'm in a halfway house.

"'Okay. I'll come pick you up in a certain area.' Dat means she done been dere before. She know exactly where to pick me up. I tryin' to play naïve, like I don't know what's goin' on, but I know. She done meet someone else at dat halfway house or dat area.

"So the first time I met her, she take me to the treatment program. Dis what made me like her. She got down dere on duke, the first day, in the car. I like'ded dat. Dat was a different flush dat I didn't understand. I already been in the penitentiary for a year and a half. So by me bein' a street guy, I already know I ain't the first one she did dat for. I didn't care. So I go to my program. She came back in an hour. She bought me a can a Pepsi pop and five dollars.

"What we call dat: she buyin' what she want. It was a

little cheap, but it was a little thing dat show the love part. Dat made me feel good. We gonna go home. She say she wanna stop at her house. Quite naturally, my own crazy thinkin' and duke, well, I might get a shot. And dat's what happened. She gave me a piece of pie dat same day. I fell for dat. I like'ded dat. I had like a year to go in the halfway house.

"Debbie from the halfway house didn't like her. She said she know she a night girl. She say she's a hoe. But guys don't care. Guys don't look at 'em as a hoe. I look at 'em dis way. She doin' what dey wanna do, what make her feel good. But womens have deir own choice, but a man have his choice, too. I feel dat kind'a womens ok with me. I stayed with her. I get outta the halfway house. I have a job. I'm workin' in the restaurant, Bob Evans. We had a pretty good time. I help payin' her bills. I was bein' responsible.

"I never forget, she listen to dis song of Boys to Men: "Over the Rainbow." All the time we had sex, she played dat. But all the time she talk about her man was in jail."

"You knew this?"

"I knew it. Because she was still in love with dis guy in jail.

"He told her he didn't want her. She feel less a women, like he didn't want her. What she do? She sent him money in jail. One day he got out of jail. He know how to get in the house. I'm in bed with my boxers on. She went to a convention. She was a nurse. She was gone outta town. I see dis guy comin' in the house. He cookin' breakfast in the kitchen for his kids. He knock on the door and axed me did I want any breakfast. I could'a got up and make an ass of myself, but I did like a player supposed to.

"My momma say don't fight over women. As bad as I want to fight, I get up and put my pants on, and I smoke me a joint.

"He said, 'Mary is my baby's momma.'

"'Okay.' I say, 'How you get in the house?'

"'Oh I always know how to get in the house. Dis is my house. She been writin' me letters all the time you all been together. The Boy to Men, she must be playin' dat record for you when you had sex? Dat's the first day I met her I play dat song.'

"I say, 'Oh, okay.'

"Den my feelin' start catchin up with me. I'm a long way from home. I'm still in Chicago, but I'm in Champagne, Illinois. I end up still on parole, so I been playin' smart. We sit up and smoke some weed and we talk'ded. So she come home. She, me, and him talkin'. We went and picked up the kids, me and him. I'm doin' what a player supposed to do. Why not fight? We gotta share and share. We pick up the kids, and dey glad to see deir dad. I can't do nothin' 'bout dat. Now she shocked. She see dese two black mans in here. Now she gotta choose. But she don't have to choose. She already know who she want. I was just the substitute, takin' care a the problem, her needs, until he got out."

"But you had to know that? You knew he was in there."

"I knew he was still in her life. When someone tell you, dey ain't seein' dis guy no more, you kind'a believe 'em, but you still don't kind'a believe 'em. Because I been drinkin' and druggin' all my life, so I still put my force field up because Lucy – an old girl friend – in Chicago, she the one burned me bad. Lina burned me real bad not to trust 'em, too. So I went along with it.

"I came out and say, 'What you gonna do about dis problem?'

"She say, 'Dats my babies daddy. He ain't got a place to stay. He can stay here. I wrote him a letter.'

"The guy already told me she wrote him a letter.

"'You mean all dis time you be writin' him a letter.'

"She say, 'No.'

"She lied to me in front of him. He already know; he told me. So I go along with it.

"She say, 'I'm gonna have my babies daddy stay here.'

"So I was hurt, really pissed, but I went along with it.

"Den turn around, we had a conversation. We went outside. He say, 'I'm goin' over to my mother's house for a week. I'm gonna give you a week ta leave.'

"I can't fight 'im. Ain't no sense to fight 'im. Me and her go in a room and discuss it. She tellin' me I can stay dere. He already told her, don't let me stay dere. She already tell me I can stay dere for a week, until I get my paycheck, den leave. I was so hurt, I packed all my things. I had dis robe, black and red. She used to wear it all the time.

"Before I left she say, 'Can I have it?'

"I say, 'No.' So he can wear my robe? 'I'll give you dis quilt I bought,' 'cause I couldn't carry it. What happened, I end up goin' gettin' high dat day."

"You were clean before that?"

"Yeah, I was clean. I was just smokin' weed. And I lost everythin': nice gold necklace, a ring, some clothes, some shoes, all the stuff I had in jail. I even had twenty-eight hundred dollars. I even help her pay the rent, try to help get on her feet. She get paid every two weeks. She always act like she's broke."

"You said she was a nurse."

"Yeah, she was a nurse. She was makin' good money. I don't know, she might'a been goin' to school for a nurse, whatever. She was gettin' a paycheck every two weeks."

"Was she a black woman or white woman?"

"White women. I stopped datin' black womens after 1988 when I start gettin' on drugs."

"How come?"

"I ain't sayin' dere ain't no nice fine womens, I just didn't wanna be bothered with the bull shit. White girls dey a little easy. Black women give you alotta fuckin' drama, and dey will fight with ya. White girls just cry and all dis shit. A black women say, 'I'll whip your ass' and all dis and dat. Plus I was hurt by 'em, and I didn't wanna be bothered. Plus dey was ghetto womens, womens hangin' out in the street. I ain't sayin' dere ain't no nice black womens out dere. I had a few of 'em, but dey tore me down so bad, dat I push myself away."

"Those two women you mentioned, Lucy and Lina?

"Right.

"Den I said to myself. I try a white women. Den another reason I try a white women is dat a white kid told me one time, I don't know if he's lyin' or not. He say, 'My daddy say a white man can get any women he want.' And I told him he couldn't. I can have any women I want, too. The reason I say dat is his sister like'ded me, and she was nice. She used to take her lunch money and buy me stuff. We had a good time. Her brother didn't like dat a black guy talkin' to his sister. I didn't give a fuck. She didn't give a fuck, excuse by my French. It was more of a hurt when someone told me I can't have somethin'.

"Den as I got a little older, my mother told me I liked white womens. And I say, 'I like all womens.' She say, 'You prefer white womens before you prefer black womens.' And from dat day, dat's what I been doin'. Once I got a little older, dey all the same, but dey think a little different. Dey see what a women see. Dey think a little different. Dey still have a guy call 'em crazy name – call 'em a bitch. Even though dey ain't gonna call no guy a crazy name, a guy still gonna call a women a crazy name. Don't care if you black, white, green, or purple, it's just a guy. Dat's the reason why."

Chapter 9

Willie's First Time in the Dane County Jail

~~~~~~

"Now I'm still working at Labor Ready. One day I get a ticket – a job – for Olive Garden bakery. Peoples came from all around the world remodelin' Olive Garden. I was workin' nights for Labor Ready.

"One mornin' I tell the contractor, let me get a job with you-all so I can travel the world.

"Dey said, 'No.'

"He had a young kid no more den eighteen, but he was a friend of the family. He didn't know nothin' much about carpentry, but I know a little more den he did, I assume.

"He said, 'I just hired dis young kid. He's a friend of the family.'

"I say to myself, white folks always helpin' white folks. You know deir prejudice.

"The next day, he tell Dave about me. And Dave came and interviewed me on the job. He was doin' concrete work on the job at Olive Garden. He had his own asphalt business.

"When I met him outside, he asked me if I knew how to use a jackhammer and a compressor.

"I tell him, 'Yeah, I do.'

"He tell me ta be dere at five o'clock in the mornin'.

"I say, 'Okay.'

"He said, 'My supervisor Bubba gonna be dere, too. I want you to bust up dis concrete.'

"But Bubba didn't never show up. Me havin' street knowledge and bein' a hustler, I knew how to run a compressor and a jack hammer, so I did it myself.

"Next day when Dave came in, he was really impressed of my work, so he started payin' me ten dollars an hour.

"Dat's how I ended up havin' the job I have today, right now.

"As I start workin' for the asphalt company, I started gettin' nice paychecks for ten dollars an hour. I'm over forty hour a week, and I still got my apartment and dis and dat.

"One day my street knowledge kick in heavy on me. I started gettin' lonely. I want me a girlfriend 'cause me and dis girl I'm seeing already fell out.

"Now I'm sayin to myself, I need a piece a pie. I go out in the street again, and I looked for a piece a pie.

I go on Park Street, on Badger, by the beltline. So I see

all the people I used to hang out with, drinkin', druggin', where all the pimps are. But dey really ain't like Chicago.

"When you meet a women, I ax if she workin', and she say, 'Yeah.' Den you tell her how much you want. And she turn around and say – dis is how I tell the womens weren't on nothin' – she say, 'I want drugs first before we have sex.'

"See, in Chicago, dey say, 'Give me my money and I can buy my own drugs. Here dey wanted drugs. So I went along with it for a couple times.

"Den the third time I went out dere again, I got caught. I relapsed. See, I had already had relapsed way back den because I was still drinkin' and smokin' pot, but I hadn't used cocaine yet. It was just a matter a time before I used cocaine again.

"So as dat happened, I meet dis girl. She want some dope.

"I say, 'I want some pie.'

"She say, 'No, I wanna get some drugs first.'

"'Okay, let's go get drugs.'

"We get in my car. We by the drug store. She in the car smokin' with me. I ain't smokin' but she is.

"So dat old behavior kicked in, and I say, 'Give me some.'

"So I took some. Dat was the biggest mistake I did.

"Took some of what?"

"Crack cocaine. Now I done relapsed again, all over

again. I cut down on my weed and on my drinkin', and I start back smokin' dope.

"Now I'm ready to hook up with dis girl all the time.

"Everytime I get paid my check be five hundred, six hundred, seven hundred dollars, and I'd blow it all in one night, and the next day I'd have to go to work. I be sick the next day and wasted all dat money on drinkin' and druggin' and cocaine and just only had sex. And I be tired, but I went to work.

"Den I had to borrow some money from my boss all over again.

"He said, 'Man, I just paid you. What happened?'

"I tell him the truth. I spent it on drinkin' and druggin'.

"He say, 'I been dere, too. But I ain't spent all my money.'

"He give me about fifty dollars. I still go out dat Saturday and spend the money again. I know Sunday I have to go to work, 'cause I work seven days a week. Dis time I played a little smart. I went home and took some of my roommate's food and made me some lunch.

"Dis goin' on for like six or seven months doin' the same behavior, gettin' high, drinkin' and druggin'.

"So when winter come, I get laid off. I'm doin' the same thing, drinkin' and druggin', gettin' high, gettin' treated like shit.

"One day, I met a friend dat I know. He asked me did I know where to get some drugs.

"I tell him, 'Yeah.'

"So we get some drugs and dis and dat.

"We run up on a girl name Denise. I heard of her, but I didn't really know her. Denise get some drugs, and she ripped him off fifty dollars of drugs. So I was pissed and he was pissed.

"I said, 'Let's go to one of my guys.'

"So we went to one of my guys and we got us some drugs.

"Den we had sa'more money. It wasn't my money, it was his money. He had seventy-five in cash and seventy-five in a winning ticket.

"I had my car, and we parked in a hotel. Dis white guy go in the bathroom with dis brother. Dis brother give him a bag of aspirin. The brother took a hundred and fifty dollars from dis guy and gave him a bag a aspirin. See the white boy was dumb because he didn't check it.

"I get pissed. I say, man you sit up here, you let somebody beat us outta dis money. Why didn't you give me the money. I was so mad, angry. I was pissed. 'Come on man, let's go home.'

"Somehow my street instincts kicked in. I see the guy who just ripped us off in dis car with the girl. So we drove up to dis gas station where he was at.

"I tell the guy, 'Man, give us half of the money and you take half ta get high. We'll solve the problem. We wanna get high just like you.'

"So the guy tried to get smart, so I swunged on him. He ducked and ran. So I chased him around the car. The girl in the car, she say, 'Get in the car.' So dey drove off.

"So I tell the guy who's sittin' next to me, 'Man, put your seatbelt on. I'm gonna kill dis mother fucker.'

"So we chased the mother fucker down the beltline. I hit dis guy four times with my car. I tried to kill 'em.

"The car blow out a flat tire, so the girl call the cops.

"Crazy as I was on dat behavior, dat drinkin' and druggin', angry from the street life, hustlin' and hurtin' somebody because dey hurt me and take somethin' from me, I was willin' to do somethin'.

"I parked the car and ran up to 'im again.

"I say, 'Man, you give me my money or I'm gonna mess fuck you up right here.'

"The guy say, 'Man, she called the cops.'

"So the guy who was sittin' in my car, he get out and ran. I say, 'Fuck it,' and I get in my car and I leave.

"The police catch me down Badger road. I had a quarter bag of weed on my arm rest.

"So when the police stop me he say, 'What's goin' on here?'

"'Nothin'.'

"'Come on, man, tell me the truth. What's goin' on?'

"'Nothin'.'

"'Dats not what dat lady said. You hit her.'

"'I'm gonna tell you just like dis, man. Dem mother

fuckers robb'ded me.' I said, 'Dey took a hundred fifty dollars from me. I say, 'I ain't lyin'. Go in deir pocket.'

"'Dey say dats deir money.'

"I say, 'Dey lyin'.'

"'He say you hit dem.'

"'No, it was a drug deal went bad.'

"'Dis here is a bad drug area around here, so I can imagine what you say.' But he say, 'Dey called in. We gotta take you to jail.'

"I had on some long-john overall pants, dirty, ripped, with paint, and greasy with oil.

"I say, 'Fuck it. Take me to jail. I don't give a fuck.'

(These words flow out of Willie's mouth like he just said them yesterday, full of spit and vinegar.)

"Dat's the first time I ever been in Dane County Jail.

"And when I get dere, the police don't never bring the quarter bag a weed in the jail to book me with. He did never bring it. He kept the weed for his self. It was some good skunk weed. So when he kept it for his self, dat show me, everywhere you go you always got crooked cops.

"I get booked in. Dey charge me with reckless endangerment – dat's hittin' people. I didn't know how the system was. I kept tellin' the people it was self-defense. "Dey tell me dere ain't no self-defense law down here unless you get beat real bad.

"I tell 'em, 'I don't let nobody hit me. If you hit me, I gonna hit you back.'

"The next day I get a signature bond. The judge let me

go. He told me, 'Stay away from dese people and dat guy right dere.'

"I get out and get to work. I call my boss and tell him I'm runnin' late because I gettin' outta jail.

"He say, 'Okay.'

"I had a court date, so I slowed down drinkin' and druggin'. If dey got my Illinois record, how dangerous I was of my behavior, I would'a got locked up.

"When I ready to go to court, a lawyer came to me and told me to take four months and he break the case down.

"I kept tellin' him, 'I ain't takin' no four months for somethin' I didn't do. It was self-defense. I only defended myself.' But Wisconsin's crooked law didn't see it dat way.

"I can deal with a guy who is straight up. The lawyer was crooked, and I know he crooked. He sit around tellin' me he doin' the right thing, but he's a crook just like me, but he's doin' it in a different fashion.

"I say, 'No.'

"I got a different lawyer.

"So dey appoint me to a public defender named Bill. Dis mother fucker was a sellout. What I mean, a sellout? He work for the system. He a fuckin' crook.

"So now the people who I hit, she didn't come to court when dey subpoena her the first time. So the second time she didn't show up again. So dey subpoenaed her a third time, and she didn't show up the third time. Dis is supposed to be the law; if someone don't show up when dey subpoena dem the third time, dey suppose to throw the case out. But my crooked lawyer, he didn't stand up to the judge and say, 'We feel the clients not responsible. She's not comin' ta court."

(It sounds like Willie's been in this situation before or he's read some law books. At this point in our working relationship I have no idea how many times Willie has been in jail in Chicago. I find out later that it was a lot! Willie is also learning how the laws in Illinois might be different than the laws in Wisconsin. He knew the Chicago system up and down. He knew what he could and couldn't do, what he could get away with. This is a new place, with new rules, and Willie doesn't like it.)

"So what my lawyer did was give her another court date, and she did show up.

"In Illinois, if dey didn't show up the first two times, dey throwed the case out.

"What Wisconsin did dis time, when the girl had to come to court, dey locked her up to testify against me in court. Dat was supposed to been thrown out. Dat show you how crooked dey is, of the system of Wisconsin. Dey didn't want you to leave the system and beat the case, and dey charge the tax payer all dis money of time dey wastin'. Dey could'a throwed it out, but dey wasted alotta tax payer money.

"She come to court. She didn't remember. She don't know nothin'. She don't know my name. She said I had on some scrappy pants, but I had on some pants with paint dat I had to work in.

"The judge say, dat's a reasonable doubt to bar me over, to take me to a higher court – to go to trial. She unreliable. And he gave her all des many chances, three times, and she didn't show up and he still gonna bar me over?

"My lawyer tell me, 'You tried to hurt somebody.'

"I say, 'What about dey tried to hurt me?'

"So he was goin' with the system because he was a public defender.

"As dat happen, my lawyer get me six months in Dane County Jail and three years a probation. He had me to cop out.

"The way dey treatin' me now, I know dey gonna treat me real bad if I take it to trial. So by me havin' the street knowledge and been through the system in Chicago, I know when to just cop out. So I just went on to cop out. So dat's my first time bein' in the system.

"Den when I did get to six months, I found out dat Dane County Po-lices talk to people like dey was crap. See the lawyers, dey couldn't talk to you like dat. Dey had to have a little respect.

"Dere was one certain lady harassed me in dere, a lady who worked dere. She had a way of pickin' on peoples and throwin' her weight around.

"I gave her a piece of my mind. I say, 'You don't talk to me like dat.' I called her a name, so she wrote me a ticket, and she tried to stop me from bein' an inmate worker.

"See, I know alotta tricks, bein' in the system, how to get outta jail.

"She harass'ded all the inmates. She push her authority around because she knew she could do dat. She know she had backup. See, in Chicago, we could'a probably slapped the mess outta her and got away with it. You could say it was self-defense. In Dane County dey have a code dat the officer is always right.

"And she kept on talkin' crap to me. I was gonna write up a grievance, like a complaint, but I just blowed it off. Every ninety days dey change deputies. So she changed at dat time.

"As I was in Huber, I was goin' out to work every day. Dave got me out every day so I could work. So I was goin' to work, doin the right thing. And one day, I relapse comin' from the job. I went and got high.

"So I left Huber. Den I turned myself back in. Dey locked me back up, and I lost my Huber for a couple days.

"By dat time it's about time for me to leave.

"I was on probation. I end up livin' at Port St. Vincent. I was still workin' for the asphalt company. Dis is where I met your brother at.

"I was walkin' down Williamson St. I had on some long-johns, short pants, and a sweat shirt. I had some boots, but my boots wasn't tied.

"I say, 'Hey man do you need any help?' I seen him come out of Ace Hardware.

"Earl say, 'Yeah I need some help. When do you wanna start?'

"I say, 'I start tomorrow.' It was the weekend.

"Your brother buildin' houses.

"He seen black peoples, but he didn't really know a black person. He seen 'em on TV and on the street, but he didn't know how crazy we was. But we all ain't crazy, but he only ran across the crazy one dat is me. He ain't never communicate with one, close-up range. Once he get to know me, he knew I was a crazy mother fucker.

"I had a few rollers drop me some medicine off. Dope dealers I call rollers. Dey livin' good, livin' large off your expense, and you live off deir expense.

"Dere was dis particular guy, I don't wanna say his name. Earl didn't like him at all. He used to drop me weed off. At dat time I slowed down smokin' cocaine when I got outta jail. I substitute one drug for another drug.

"I had a probation officer [PO] named Pat. I liked dat probation guy. He was good and responsible guy, and I took him as one of my best friends.

"We had a neighborhood cop named Jane. I still liked her, too. Her and Pat were friends. And I liked the both of dem. I still like both of dem today. She was a wonderful lady.

"She was the one dat start teachin' me dat all cops ain't bad. My thinkin' is all cops is the same. She start teachin' me a different way, dat dey only doin' dere job. I start to like her as who she was, a human bein'.

"Pat was my agent. Pat lost his position. Somebody else took over his job.

"I moved from Port St. Vincent to one of the Lazy Jane buildin's. When I move in dere, I see a guy come out the window.

"A young kid was livin' dere. He was shootin' dope. He had some of his dope friends dere. How dey got in, dey go through the window.

"The guy downstairs, he called the cops.

"One day the cops asked me, 'How I feel the guy break into your apartment.'

"I say, 'He didn't break into my apartment.'

"The cop told me, 'He want me to come and testify.'

"I told him, 'I don't fuck with cops. I don't like cops. I don't come and testify for nothin'.'

"So the cop tell me he gonna tell my probation agent.

"I say, 'Tell my probation agent, I don't give a fuck.'

"I had a new probation agent. He thought he was a tough cookie.

"Jane, she heard about it.

"I tell her, 'I don't like cops. I ain't gonna go nowhere.'

"My probation agent, he tried to be hard. All the time he start comin' to my house. One day he came to my house to drop me.

(Dropping means having to take a urine test for drugs or a "piss test," as Willie describes it.)

"I just got done smokin' weed. I had a roommate dat was one of his clients. He end up droppin' my roommate, den me. He smelled the weed in the apartment.

"I said, 'Dat's my weed.' All the time I have four joints rolled up on my dresser.

"Jane overlooked dat. My PO wanted to lock me up, but Jane told him don't lock me up. Dat was a good thing. She didn't see me goin' to jail for nothin' like dat. All dat time she play like she didn't see the joints.

"The next day he said I had to do some volunteer work. I had to do some volunteer for Willy Street fair. I had to tear down a stage.

"From dere, me and my PO got on bad terms. I got another roommate. His name was Jim, an older guy. He thought he was slick. I think he was gay cause Wisconsin got alotta gay fuckin' men.

"One day I was gettin' high. He axed me if I knew where to get some drugs at, not marijuana, cocaine.

"I told him, 'Sure I know where to get some cocaine.'

"'How 'bout some rock?'

"'Sure I know how to get some of dat, too.'

"So he gave me fifty dollars. So I went and got him some drugs.

"He wanted to smoke 'em [the rocks of cocaine]. So I had to make a pipe for him, and we ended up smokin' 'em together.

"As I start smokin', I say, 'Man, we got a get us some ladies.' We got some more money outta the bank. I see dis girl name, think her name was. . . I forgot what her name was. I ax her does she get high?

"She say, 'Yeah.'

"I told her up front. I told her what the game was before she get in the car. I told her we wanna have sex, we wanna train on [two guys with one woman in the middle]. I want some of dat pie. So she went along with it.

"She say, 'Okay.'

"So as we go to the crib, she was given us some head. Jim couldn't get hard, so he was mad.

"She say, 'Dat boy won't get hard, Willie.'

"I say, 'Dat's his problem. I'm gettin' hard.' So she did me.

"Den I got a piece of dat pie. And Jim was mad. He was sittin' in the chair playin' with his self, tryin' to get his self off. I didn't care what he was doin'

"So we needed sa'more dope. He give me two hundred dollars to buy sa'more dope.

"I told Donna, 'You stay here with Jim.' She stayed dere with him. I get two hundred dollars of dope – two eight balls.

"When I came back, I said, 'Did you give 'em a piece of dat pie.'

"She say he just wanna eat it.

"I say, 'Dat's cool.'

"So we start smokin' again. As we start smokin', we start freakin' off all over again."

"Is this women black or white?"

"She's white.

"She was good at what she did. Matter-a-fact I fell for her a little bit.

"Jim mad. He still can't get hard. As dat happen he say he gonna go to bed.

"I say, 'Okay man, I'm gonna take her home.'

"He say, 'You can use my car.'

"So he had a Cadillac. He let me use it to take her home, but I didn't take her home.

"I said, 'Look here, if you still wanna get high, you have to make some money.'

"She said, 'Okay.'

"I turned her on to a couple dates. So we made a little money.

"So I go to dis bar, and I run into dis guy.

"He say, 'Man, where the womens at?'

"I say, 'What? I know, I got one for ya. We can have a good time.'

"See, he wanna be a dope dealer. He had alotta drugs dat night. He maybe had a thousand dollars worth a drugs and money and whiskey. We partied. We go to his crib and start partyin'

"Now he got a problem. He kind'a ashamed havin' another man in front of him seein' him gettin' some head.

"I told him, 'Man, don't be ashamed a me. She gonna take care a bof'a us. She already know the room, so you don't gotta be ashamed.'

"I told her to get naked. And she get naked. Dat turned me on. She did what I want her to do.

"I say, 'You gonna give him some right dere on the couch. I get high while you give some.'

"So she did.

"Now I got involved into it together with it myself. She was givin' some head, and I was givin' it from the back. Dat's a fantasy I always love. We had a good time.

"He tried to keep her for himself. But all the time she was my girl, bein' with me. What we call, dat's your hustler. She was hustlin' with me. I gotta look out for her. She doin' what I want her to do.

"As dat happen, me and her started hangin' out. We stayed in the house for two days. After dem two days, he say he want another girl.

"So I go find dis other girl. I leave her with him. He didn't do nothin' to her. I don't know what des guys be thinkin'. He didn't do nothin' to her.

"I find another girl. She a lot slicker den he was. I seen her before, and she had a tattoo down dere by her pie. I told her to get naked. She was sexy. The foursome started ta party.

"Now he fell in love with the second girl. He wanna take her along in the back and dis and dat, right?

"After we been dere two days, now he want me and Donna to leave.

"I tell Donna, 'So what. We can leave.'

So we left, and I took my roommate car back. My roommate called the cops while I was out and say dat I stole his car and took his bank book and wrote checks.

"So the po-lice locked me up. My PO get a statement from me. He say your roommate say you rob 'im and wrote a check.

"I said, 'Man, I'm gonna tell you the truth, I didn't do none of dat shit. I was gettin' high, smokin' dope, but he went to the bank his self, all you have to do is look at the cameras. Dat'll tell you he was lyin' to the police.'

"Dey didn't do nothin' to him. Dey could of gave him an obstructed justice ticket. Show you how crooked the cops is.

"My PO lock me up and send me to Oak Hill, and I went to prison dat day.

All through this Willie keeps talking about getting his "pie." He only thinks of women as sex objects, "not all womens," – he wants to be fair – but most of them. He's told me many times how he's been burned by women, and now all he wants from them is sex. He doesn't want any relationship, and he tells them that.

Well, at least he's upfront with them, I think.

And he starts to talk about if he had sex with me. Even though he uses his pie euphemism, it bothers me when he directs this kind of talk at me. I'm glad that we're sitting in a busy restaurant. He says he wouldn't do that though because he has respect for my mother and for Earl.

"Your brother would beat me up."

"Yeah, right after my husband and right after me!"

We always meet where other people are at and when he's sober and straight, so I really don't think Willie would push himself on me. But if he was on drugs or drunk, that would be a different matter. So I tell him.

"Listen Willie. This is a professional relationship. You gotta respect that. If you don't..."
"Yeah, I know. It means alotta money." (He half chuckles.)
"That's right! You'd lose alotta money."

The waitress that Willie stopped to talk to as we were sitting at the table is now at the checkout. So as we leave he saunters up to her and stands as close as the desk lets him, leaning into toward her as he asks what she's been up to etc...

I think as I watch him do his thing, *Sex is going to be his downfall. He likes it too much, and he gets it in all the wrong places, usually with women who use. Just like the story he told me today. I really question whether Willie is really going to be able to make it "clean and sober" because of his obsession with sex and how that is tied to drug use, in his case.*

I also hope it doesn't end up getting him killed.

Later, after I've dropped him off and he has shown me the paint work he's doing on my aunt's apartment, he gives me a very brotherly hug goodbye.

He tells me, "You know, you almost a sister."
"What do you mean?"

"A sister is a friend."

"A girl once tol' me, if you with a girl for six or nine months and you ain't had her pie, den you just friends. You almost dere."

He says this as he looks down, almost in defeat. It looks like he doesn't want to admit it just yet, but I think he finally understands the truth of the situation.

I get in the car and sigh. It's a relief to know he finally understands that very important fact. It gives me hope that maybe we can meet and he won't try and flirt with me each and every time.

What am I thinking? Willie will always flirt with me; that is Willie: a flirt. But hopefully just not as much if I'm his "sister."

CHAPTER 10
Relapse

I meet Willie at his house on Sherman Avenue. I find out that he is in charge of the house he is currently living in, making sure things get done and everyone does the jobs they're supposed to do. He's at a place called Oxford house. There are many of these homes all across the country. The organization describes themselves as a "democratically run, self supporting, drug free home." Willie enjoys being here, most of the time, anyway. He likes the freedom and the home environment. He heard about this place on the street. He filled out an application, then was interviewed by the people living there at the time. They decided Willie could join them. He has a DVD that explains how Oxford House got started. He puts it in for me to watch. He starts talking about his responsibilities as the head of the house.

"I don't push no issue, because I try an work with 'em, 'cause everybody have feelin's. I want dem to get to know me, not just sayin' I'm your mom or your dad or dis or dat. No, dis is your responsibility. Dat's what we get in trouble with, everybody tellin' us what ta do. It's a mistake. It's not really a mistake, it's a behavior. You come in here and have a choice to live and do right. To be clean and sober. Whatever you wanna do, you can do it. Dat's life. Dat's the way it is. You can't get around it or nothin'. If you got dirty dishes, you know dey is yours. Don't let me ax you when you gonna do 'em. You deal with it. When I stand on 'em a little bit, dey get pissed, like I would.

"Like Thursday, the house was really a mess. I worked hard all day. I had to cut the grass. I had to take the trash out. I had to do all dese things, and you sit here and tell me dat you didn't have time. Dat's your responsibility. It ain't about nobody else, it's about you. If you wanna have someone tell you what to do every day, you need to go back where you at. I ain't gonna say jail, but if you go out dere, people are gonna tell you what ta do. You ain't gonna make no decision for you. If you wanna do somethin' better, show your stuff, you can do it. I ain't got no problem with you. I have a problem. It's about me. I know what I like. I do what I want.

"It don't mean you not supposed to try. Dat's what life is about; you suppose to try ta get somethin'. If you don't try to get it, you know you can get it. Dis what it's about. It's not about: I can't, I can't.

"You put me back in dat neighborhood, you back in dat same behavior. You know what you gonna do, you already know you gonna relapse. Dis what it's about: how I deal with it, how much success change my life, how I'm gonna get a job, how am I gonna get a girl. How I'm gonna do all dis. I know how. I just have to be responsible for me, not to relapse. If I relapse, dat's me not payin' attention to dat hole in the ground. You see what I'm sayin'?

"Dat's what it is. I come to dis house. It's nice. I was in a halfway house in Chicago. I know what's right and wrong.

"It's like a squirrel crossin' dat street. He already know a car. He gotta try if he gonna die doin' it. Dat's what life is about. Ain't no such thing as I can't. If you couldn't do it, you won't be in dis world.

"I got alotta knowledge under my belt. Lotta people think I don't, but I remember a time I used to have some responsible for myself. My momma didn't pay no bills. I paid the bills. She say, go pay dis bill, and I go paid it. Dat's what I'm talkin' about. I still drinkin' and druggin' though, but I responsible with her money, not with my money.

"See, I left home when I was a early, early age. I didn't wanna follow her rules. Her rules wasn't bad. I wanted to be a man and do my own thing. A woman can't teach a man how to be a man 'cause she can't; she ain't a man. A woman can teach a girl how to be a woman. You need a man to teach a man how to be a man. 'Cause if you try to teach a man to be man, you might come out with a little sugar. It's like the birds and the bees.

"And dats what relapse is. You makin' a mistake and you recognize your mistakes, you replapse, you fail. It's not even dat you a failure. I don't think anyone who drinkin' and druggin', he's not a failure. He gotta put more effort into what he wanna do. He already know what he gotta do, he just gotta do it.

"I can change. Change do come about in life when you make alotta mistakes."

"So like Friday, you tried to go to a movie, it got late and you gave up."

"See, I'm a movie freak. Say I went to the movie. I had a hundred some dollar in my pocket. So I would walk to catch the bus. I would have to go past the neighborhood dat I have to ride the bus through. And it was Friday, and I already had the jumpin' urge in me of relapsin'. I would have got off the bus to use. I didn't care about the place or none a dis. I would'a relapsed. Dat's why I axed for support. I axed for it in a way I ain't never axed for it before.

"I used to not being responsible. I would have say fuck it. Let me go out and get high. Ease the pain 'cause it abuse you very bad. Just like any addiction you have, it abuse you so bad. You thinkin', 'I'm tired of gettin' beat up, let me just go on and fuckin' do it.' I know if I would a go ahead and did it, it would have been a different story. I would say 'Wow, I done fucked up again.' Den I might'a not come home.

"Matter-a-fact, I got dis debit card. I got like fourteen hundred dollars in the bank. Dat would a been pissin' down the drain.

"My goal is to get me a car. I would'a lost my goal again. And some people just say, 'Fuck it,' like I did once before. I had eighteen hundred dollars, and I thought I was in love with dis dumb bitch. But I gonna keep it real with you. If I don't keep it real with you, in dis book, in my life here, den I won't be true to me.

"I make dat decision to be with her. I don't really fault her, but I fault myself that I got used. Even though I know she used me, and I was usin' her, and I know drinkin' and druggin' was in dere, too."

"Is this the Cuban girl?" (Willie had told me about a Cuban girl he hooked up with when he got out of jail recently.)

"Yeah. Dats the relapsin' dat I didn't pay attention to. And I let my feelin' and my thinkin' guidin' my way. I didn't want dat to happen again. Dat was the issue of dat.

"Addiction is a very strange thing. If you addicted, it can be a good addiction, it can be a bad addiction. Like some people, dey constantly read, dey pick up everythin' and read. It's an addiction, too. Like some people go into the store and take stuff. Like Paris Hilton. She get caught with a quarter ounce a cocaine in her purse, and her behavior tell her dat ain't her's. Dat an addiction. Dat is her purse and you tellin' me it's not. Dat's an addiction. She get caught right dere and her drinkin' and druggin' behavior tell her dat ain't her's. Dat's what relapsin's all about. And you try to figure out how to change it."

"You went to the store, came home, then went to bed."

"I came home and still tried to watch a movie. I was so tired I don't even watch the movie. I slept on the couch for a little while. Den I went to the room and went to bed and went to work the next day. I got up at four and went back to sleep. I set the clock for like five, den I went to sleep. I got up about five thirty, got ready and went to work."

"You said Saturday you still felt like using."

"All day Saturday, I didn't have no problem. See, when a person don't have nothin' to do with your time, when you first tryin' to get clean and sober, the first thirty days is a detriment. What I mean is dat you don't wanna use, but you wanna use.

"See I got a little clean time under my belt. But what made me wanna use is my boss tellin' me I had to leave early, at two thirty. My thinkin' is, you got all dis clean time, you ain't got nothin' to do with yourself. So what I did, I start callin' peoples. Like Mike, he's my mentor; he's like my sponsor, too. Den I called Sam, he's like my sponsor.

Den I called your brother Earl. And I called Earl, and he call back. Dese guys help me when I'm feelin' bad, when I'm feelin' really down and I'm upset.

"And another thing dat make me upset, dis guy, he got my bicycle, and he haven't returned my bike, 'cause I gotta put it in the shop to get it fixed. And when my boss tell me, I could'a worked until eight if I have my license. Dat made me mad.

(Willie's talking about his driver's license, which he doesn't have right now. I don't know how he lost it but my guess is because of DUIs.)

"I came home Saturday. On my way home I call dese people 'cause I got alotta free time. I don't know what to do with myself. I called Earl. Earl say he at the grocery store.

Earl is closer to Willie than I am. I first met Willie at my mother's four or five years ago. Earl would bring Willie over to my mother's for an occasional Sunday meal. Earl must have told Willie that I was a writer, and the minute he heard that fact, in his mind, I had already written his book. Willie had been working for Earl, helping him with his work projects, for at least a year before I met him. Earl is single, as Willie is, so I think they like doing things with each other on occasion, like going to movies. It might also help that Earl doesn't drink or smoke.

"I say, 'Would you like to go to the movie?'

"He say, 'Sure, I like to go see *Stock Market*.'

"Dat ain't my kind'a movie. I just like movies straight out, you gonna kill, you gonna rob, don't sit around and play mind games. So he thought the movie start at five thirty.

"What happen was, the movie dat he wanna see started at five thirty, den he went down the hall to see the movie. I went to the bathroom, and I didn't know where he went. I didn't know dey had two of dem goin'. So I'm sittin' around. I see his car out dere. I don't wanna take the bus 'cause it'd go by the neighborhood [the bad neighborhood where Willie could get drugs]. So I started callin' people to come pick me up. See dat relapse thinkin' still goin on in me. So I started usin' my cell phone. I got in touch with Mike and Sam. Dey say dey can't do nothin'. I went back in the theater and watch part of a movie, *Resident Evil*; it was a video game. It was crap. So I walked out and Earl call me on my cell phone, and he told me he was ready to go. And I was glad of dat.

"So I got home last night about eight. I came home. I watched some of the movie dat I bought. I fixed me some dinner. I had some rice, some cube steak, and had me a big glass a tea. And I sat here on the couch and went to sleep again. Den I got up Sunday. I'm feelin' good. I listen to my music. I wanna cut some grass. I suppose to go to a meetin' today, but I didn't wanna hang out with dem guys 'cause I had got my blood pressure up little bit 'cause I'm still havin' dis behavior of relapsin' in my mind. I don't want no one to tell me what to do now. Let me make my own decisions. If I need some help, I will get some help from you. I will ax you for some help.

"Once upon a time, I ain't never axed no man for no help. 'Cause I feel dat in my drinkin' and druggin' days dat I can do it myself, but you can not do dis by yourself. When you an addict, you always need some help. Plus I pray every mornin', too, and I ask God and thank 'im. And every day before I go to sleep, I thank 'im for wakin' me up, and for doin' dis right for me. Dat's part of it.

"Another thing I did Friday. I went and bought some boots. My roommate take me to Walmart to buy some boots. I bought me another watch, pay my cell phone bill, and I went grocery shoppin'. Dat's how I deal with it.

"And dat's how my day went. Today I thought about you, too. I don't want to make my appointment with you and go out and fuck up, den it all goin' down the drain. Dat's how I'm startin' to think. The key of bein' clean and sober is your eyes and your thinkin' 'cause your eyes see alotta things.

"Sometime you can be blind, you really don't see, but you see, but your thinkin' runs around so many ways. You say, 'Let me try dis, it ain't gonna hurt.' It might not hurt. It's your curiosity, you wanna see just like every other human bein' to see what life is about. Dat's what an addict do."

"Have you gotten on the computer here yet?"

"Don't ask me about usin' the computer. I don't use dat mother fucker at all. It don't excite me. To me it's bad. It's a good thing, but it's bad. It's nosy. You give your information away, and someone take it and use it. Some use it as a tool for bad things. You put so much'a your experience and your time in dere, people can just describe who you really are and what you do, 'cause it can get dem all dis information.

"I don't have the ability to sit down and do it. It's ain't my cup a tea. I don't' see the interest in it."

"All right. That's all right."
(Time to give up on my original plan that Willie type up some of his story himself. Ah, the best made plans...)

"I'm hands on, anythin' I do. If I do it, I make sure I touch it or see it. When I out dere drinkin' and druggin', you don't sell me drugs if I don't see it. I don't say it don't happen to me. I done got burnt like dat. I done get beat outta a hundred dollars.

"I got in trouble once like dat before. Someone sold me some asprin. I tol' you about dat already. I hit 'em with my car, three times. I might a killed 'em.

"I did somethin' right dere on the spot. If you don't take care of 'im den and dere, it ain't no good no more. If you deal with it right dere on the spot, it's easy 'cause your anger already dere and your violence already dere. Den you show your expression like an animal. You don't care if you live or die. Just like dat squirrel. He wanna get across the street. He know he can get over dere, he done

done it before and it's good. But dat a choice and a thinkin' and a behavior. If I have to die to get over dere, I gonna try. Dat's the way life is."

"You wanted to tell me about a murder you saw?"

(As long as Willie has lived in a hostile environment, and even though his temper can get away from him at times, Willie doesn't consider himself a killer, and he wants people to know that. Willie also has a clear sense of justice, and getting pulled into this murder after the fact is unjust in Willie's eyes.)

"I was dere."

"When was this?"

"It was about twenty years from now. I'm livin' on the north side around Broadway and Wilson and Sheriden. I'm deep, deep into drugs. I was so deep into drugs, I didn't take baths for like three or four months. I was deep on dem drugs. Didn't sleep. Didn't do nothin'.

"Dis one day I was haggin' out on Hans and Montro. I was tryin' to get some dope. It was a sunny day. A friend a mine named Goldy, he fell in love with a girl dat get high. I don't call 'em a hoe, I call 'em night life. She get high. She have sex, whatever it takes to get drugs. What we call in the old days: Captain hoe tryin' to save a hoe.

"He was a really big dope dealer. He was what we call a roller. He was sellin' drugs outta dis house, dis apartment. He was a cool guy. He was all right, but he get high, too.

"Goldy had a young lady to stay dere with him to help get her clean and sober. He tried to help 'er, but he had the wrong intention. He might'a fell in love with her, too.

"I see him and buy dope from him, and I know the girl, too. I didn't have a chance to get her, bad as I wanted to get her, but I was too into drugs. I was livin' on the streets. I was livin' on the gangway, hallways. I didn't sleep at all. When I did sleep, I go to Chicago Uptown Ministry, the Hopper House, or the church. Chicago Uptown Ministry was on Sherman Avenue, the Hopper House was across the street. Chicago Uptown Ministry was a place where people come in, dey had a daycare. Dey help'ded peoples to get on deir feet. I know alotta good friends dere. I know the pastor. I know everybody's name and dey help me. Dey always help'ded me to go in deir and sleep, and I help'ded dem.

"People donate to help dem out. The Hopper House is a place where you can take a shower, get a change a clothes every night and rest and eat and watch movies. A guy named Simon, he was a recoverin' alcholic and an addict, he was runnin' the place. Most of the people runnin' the place, dey were recoverin' addicts. But not the Uptown Ministry. Dere was no user dere. The church was just a church, and at night at eight o'clock, everybody went to sleep until five o'clock in the mornin' or seven.

"One mornin' I see Goldy with two other peoples.

"I say, 'Hey man, you got any drugs?' I had like twenty dollars.

"And he say, 'No.' He axed me to come back.

"I say, 'ok.'

"I come back and Goldy said, 'What's up.'

"'Not much.'

"We know each other. We went to school together.

"'I know you from school.'

"We went to Crane Tech High School.

"He say, 'I want you to do somethin' for me, man. Stand down here and watch out for me.'

"So I don't really know what's going on, but I do know he sells drugs outta dis house. And he go upstairs. Goldy and two others guys, dey go upstairs. I ain't really payin' attention to what's goin' on. I'm downstairs waitin'.

"First he tells me he gonna look out for me when he come downstairs 'cause I got twenty dollars. He say he didn't have no drugs, but he gonna come back and give me some for doin' dis favor. He gonna look out for me.

"He say, 'I'm goin' upstairs and talk to dis guy.'

"Dis was the drug house. He go upstairs. It was on the third floor. I'm downstairs waitin' about one hour. He come back downstairs, him and dese other two guys. Dey in a hurry now. We walkin' toward the car, I think it was like a chevy.

"He say, 'I see you when I come back.'

"My curiosity because of my street life, my behavior, my crazy life, is dere. I went upstairs to see what's happenin'. I see two peoples dead. I go in the guy's pockets. I didn't have time to walk around and see if dere's any drugs, but I go in his pockets. He ain't had no money or nothin'. The dude was sittin' with a white tee shirt on and black pants, and the girl was sittin' right next to him.

"See, bein' in the street life, I already know Goldy was havin' sex with her. I already know dat. He acted like he didn't know, but he know. You aren't supposed to fall in love with someone who do drugs, 'cause dey unpredictable. See what I'm sayin'?

"The guy had two holes in his head. Bein' in the street I know it was a small pistol, a hand pistol or somethin' like dat. And the girl had one in her head.

"Me bein' a street life guy, I'm assumin' dis is how it went; I don't know, but dis is what I'm assumin'. See, Goldy was in love with dis girl. He wanted to take the girl off the street and make her his woman, but the code on the street say you can't take a hoe off the street and make her your wife, but you can take a house wife and make her a hoe. Dat was his first mistake.

"She was with dis other guy in dis drug house, and I think she givin' dis guy a break [for his drugs]. Dis guy sellin' drugs outta dis house for Goldy.

"The girl up dere partyin' with dis guy.

"Goldy might'a shot the girl hisself, but Goldy shot the guy to show the girl. He shot the guy to show the point."

"To the girl?"

"Yeah. 'Cause he fucked up the money, the drug money, and he with Goldy's girl.

"Goldy got juice – he got pull. Goldy told one of the guys dat be with him to shoot the girl 'cause she a witness. He had the right. Den Goldy's guy, he shot the guy too just to be shootin' him, just to show he can. See dere was three bullets. The guy had two bullets in his head. Dat's how I think it went. I was tryin' to find drugs, so I didn't pay attention. I was a dope fiend, an addict on the streets. The street life tell me to get outta here. I wiped my fingerprints off the doorknob. Dat's as far as I went. I got real scared.

"As I leavin' the buildin', I saw a lady on the left-hand side, and she looked out the door. She probably didn't pay a good attention to me, my look or my face. I looked at her and she looked at me, and I kept goin'. I just went out the buildin', and I didn't hear 'bout Goldy no more since den.

"Until 'bout ten years later, he try to put me involved in dat murder."

"Of the drug dealer and Goldy's girlfriend?"

"Right. He fell in love with a night girl. Two things dat a person dat drinkin' an druggin' know: A girl dat smoke cocaine, she not trustable. You cannot trust her at all 'cause she will steal. A girl dat do her-o-in, she gonna be so high she gonna still be in the same spot. She don't move when she high. A girl dat drink, she gonna be so drunk she gonna fall out. So dem the three things you learn about three different womens. But dey all have an addiction problem. And Goldy know dis from bein' in the street so long.

"Goldy tried to use me as an excuse dat he say he with me. He know he wasn't with me. He lie to the state and to his lawyer dat he was with me all the time about what happened with the murder. He didn't have to put my name involved in none a dat because I didn't mention his name about nothin' until dis day in the book I'm writin'.

"I talked to some FBIs and the state and some lawyer and some people who believe in some innocent people bein' locked up. You know, sometimes people go to prison and dey be innocent? Goldy ain't the one bein' innocent. He ain't no innocent victim. He is the person dat did a bad decision, a crime dat he commit, and he try to make me with it.

"The reason I ran from dat situation, I got scared. I didn't want ta be a part of dat because the street life sayin', you see and you don't see, you hear and you don't hear. Dat's the code you have in the street."

Willie is obviously pissed that Goldy tried to implicate him in some way in this murder. Willie has a strong sense of what is right and what is wrong (at least to Willie) and when someone goes against that, especially when it's a street code, a code that Goldy knew just as well as Willie, it really bothers him.

"But when he broke dat code, dats why he is in dis book today. I wouldn't a never mentioned dis situation if he would a never mentioned dat. He tried to say I was his... what dey call it, his alibi? Dis would have never been mentioned at all. I would'a took it to my grave."

"So when did you hear that he tried to make you his alibi?"

"Ten years ago. I was livin' in Madison, Wisconsin. I was stayin' at Port St Vincent. How dey found me is through my social security card.

"I had stopped workin' for over fifteen years when I was drinkin' and druggin'. I couldn't work. I didn't wanna work. When I come to Wisconsin, I got a job, and I started workin' again through Labor Ready. My social security number started poppin up. The person who was still lookin' at the case found me. Dey didn't close the case until dey found me. Dey knows I wasn't dead. Next thing you know I got a job workin' at dis asphalt place. I'm workin' every day. A family business. Dey came to my house one day and left a message sayin' deyed like to talk to me."

"Who was trying to contact you?"

"The newspaper, the po-lices, anybody in the state, and dey had deir own witness. I think the FBI be part of dat, too, 'cause it was a high murder in Chicago on the north side on Haze and Montro. Dat's why dey left a message to Port St. Vincient dat dey wanted to talk to me. I didn't know for sure what the FBI want. I know dat case had drugs. Dey was prob'ly investigatin' dat, too.

"Den dey talked to someone at Port St. Vincent and relayed a message. It was all in the newspaper, 'bout Goldy. Nobody really know who I was. Dey know my name is

Willie Lee Triplett. Goldy know my name because we went to school together. So he tell everyone what happened."

"What paper?"

"I think it was the Chicago Tribune. Goldy kept tellin' his lawyer he was innocent. Nobody in Chicago, dey don't wanna send no innocent man to jail on no double homicide murder. So dey really want to see if it's true. So he lied to dem peoples.

"See I only assume how the murder went down, but I know it went down. When he told me to look out for him, I didn't know he was gonna do dat. All I know he want to check on his drugs and his money. Bein' an addict, I know dat. I know he had a smoke house up dere."

"The FBI came, dey brought a newpaper. Dey showed me he was in the newspaper and tellin' me what Goldy said, and dey show me some pictures. I didn't know the two guys in the picture but I know Goldy.

"Dat's my first time ever bein' real real close up to a murder. I done seen people get hurt and killed and shot but not actually dead, dead. To make it so bad, the girl didn't die right dere. The girl died in the hospital. She already told 'em who it was. She told 'em who shot her. He tried to use me as a scap goat, sayin' the girl is lyin' so he didn't have to go to prison the rest of his life. If he would'a took his own way, he would have never been mentioned in dis book, period."

"So they just came and talked to you, and then they left?"

"They came and talked to me, and investigate to see if my story was true. And dey found out I was tellin' the truth. I didn't know nothin' about it. I ran just like any other person would run, 'cause I was scared. I don't wanna die. Plus I was on drugs, too. I sure wasn't gonna go and tell no po-lice. Den dey gonna ask me all dese stupid questions. No. No, I wasn't gonna do dat. I just left. I moved further north to about Cabrini Green. Den I started hangin' around Carbrini Green gettin' high."

(Willie changes gears)

"Many times in my life I tried to get clean and sober. Back den I don't never really think relapse play a big part of your recovery. Even though you don't wanna relapse, but you relapse. What I mean is, dat if you been gettin' high for some thirty some years, your mind and your body get transferred into a different thing from life. Den when I first went to a meetin', I was a rebellion, very rebellion."

"How old were you? Was this in Chicago?"

"The judge ordered me to go to the intervention treatment center. It was a six month program. The people who was runnin' it was alcohol and drug addicts. Dey were wonderful peoples. Dey had a family guy dere who was helpin'. I had a counselor there named Kyle, I'm not for sure. It was set up like a military thing, but it was a recovery thing. The six month program was about you bein' helpless.

I was about thirty-one or thirty-two when I first went into a treatment program."

"Was this after your first time in jail?"

"No. I was still goin' in and outta jail. Dis was after dat, but I did steal a car, and I got caught, and I told my lawyer I had a drug problem, so he told the judge to order me to go to treatment in Chicago. It was intervention at 5701 S. Wood St. in Chicago. When I came dere, I don't have no clothes, no nothin'. My thinkin' was to constantly get high twenty-four hours. Deir job was to get me to think better, to hold a job, be responsible, and notice my behavior. If you had conflict with anyone, dey tied you together [literally]. You had to learn how to communicate with dat individual who you don't like.

"We used to have alotta meetin's, seven days a week. We usually get up at five in the mornin', get in line. First we had to make our bed, wash our face, dis and dat. Dey was teachin' us lots'a responsible things. Tryin' to show you dat you can change. When I came in the door, my thinkin' and my behavior haven't never changed. I was constantly thinkin' of gettin' high, wantin' to do dis, wantin' to go out. I hadn't never pay attention to dat.

"You don't have to relaspe if you catch it the first time. See what I'm sayin'. But if you don't catch it, you gonna replapse. Relapse is part of recovery. But if you wanna change, you can take hold of the program, but if you don't take hold'a dat, you gonna relapse because of your thinkin' and your behavior.

"So what happened was, I was in with my counselor tellin' him about all dese problems, den dey had me to go to what dey call like welfare. We couldn't help ourselves. We didn't have no income, no nothin', no money. And dey was tryin' to get us like social security. We could get it through the program. The goverment was supplyin' it for a while and food stamps to help pay our food and rent, not only me but other guys.

"And every Wednesday dey used to have us put a shirt and tie on and show us how to go out on interviews, to talk to people and show us how to get a job. We had different counselors – anger management counselor. We talked about love, happiness, family, how to get into a different relationship. All dis in dat program. Dat was the best program I ever ever been in.

"I was dere for four months. Some people had left the program. If dey come back in three days, dey get voted back in. But if you be gone after three days, dey just pack your stuff up and give it to you at the door and you just leave.

"And dey have like a big brother in dere for you: a mentor. Everybody in dere is a mentor to help you change your thinkin' and your behavior. And the counselor did good.

"Some guys got deir GED – deir high school diploma. We worked in the kitchen downstairs, in the basement. We had group all the way to five thirty, den lunch break, den do the dishes, and we had a quiet time, too.

"My stepmother brought me some clothes over, and she done gave me some money."

"Your stepmother? I don't think I know about your stepmother?"

"Remember I told you about my stepmother. I went over to my dad's house and she didn't even know me."

"Oh yeah, yeah, now I remember, but you haven't said much about her."

"She brought me some clothes, and dats when I first came in the program. She was proud of me and everythin' and gave me some money.

"One day I asked my counselor – I was dere for four months – I ask my counselor, 'Can I go out to a movie?' He said, 'Sure.'

"The movie I wanted to go see was *Sugar Hill* with Wesley Snipes. He was a big drug dealer at the movie and his brother was a drug head, too. His dad was a he-ron shooter, and dey ain't never mentioned deir moms.

"Before I go to the movie my counselor axed me did I need some support. I thought I did had support. I thought I was strong, but I wasn't. See dat was dat same thinkin' dat I had when I was out on the street, when I was drinkin' and druggin' so long I don't never get a chance to know how to deal with it.

"So as it came about, I go to the movie. I see the movie,

and I relapse. I relapse on the movie 'cause dere was drinkin' and druggin' in dere and womens. You know I not makin' no excuse of womens be a part of drinkin' and druggin', but dey do play a part, but I do take my own responsibility of relapse dat was me 'cause of my thinkin'.

(Willie launches into his ideas about relapsing and being an addict. He rambles on quite a bit, but I've included much of it because it gives you a good idea of how he thinks about things related to his addictions. It also illustrates how important this topic is to him, similar to his interest in love. Not too surprising.)

"Relapse is dis way. First you gotta learn how it change your thinkin' about who you are. See, when you a child and you start off drinkin' and druggin' at an early age, you don't never meet dat nice person inside you 'cause you already another person, a drinkin' and druggin' person. Dat the first person you really notice was dat drinkin' and druggin' guy, dat behavior dat you see from the street life, runnin' the streets all night, partyin', hangin' out with the wrong crowd, the wrong neighborhood. And you got dat image when you young, and it stick to ya, and you start glamorizin' it, and you start likin' it. And as you start likin' it, you don't know how to see the other person inside you 'cause you hide it.

"Dat's what relapse do. Relapse make you forget somethin' dat you know dat inside'a you. You cannot find it 'cause you been drinkin' and druggin' for so long. Den once you get into dese programs, you start gettin' a taste of programs, start gettin' a taste of bein' who you are. It's another side'a you, a clean and sober person. When you was a child you ain't never experienced it, 'cause all your life you been hangin' around people who been drinkin' and druggin', partyin', goin' out, and not listenin' to your parents, not listenin' to people older, and you just stick with dat bad behavior, dat party.

"And when you go into a rehab program, dey teach you a little about you and bein' sober.

"See, alotta success peoples who been drinkin' and druggin', from my point of view bein' an addict, is dat dey struggle with it just as much as I struggle with it today. It's dat drinkin' and druggin' behavior. And you don't know how to control it until you try to figure out who you are.

"And when you go into dese programs, all dese people promise things of bein' sober, but you drinkin' and druggin', so you never believe deir promise. All you know: I'm an addict. All you know: I like to get high. All you know: I wanna feel good. Dat's all you wanna know. Your body tell you, your mind tell you, your eyes tell you, and your mouth tell you your actions. All dis tell you what you feel and what you like doin' in life. And before you notice, relapse come to you before you really relapse. What I mean is, dat is your behavior. You might get angry or you might not be payin' attention or your eyes see somethin' dat you like, dat you did before, and it bring back memories. You try and fight it off, dat it not comin' right now, but down the line, if you not payin' attention, you gonna relapse.

"My sayin' is dat I relapse all the time, but I try not to. What I mean is it's my thinkin'. I don't mean I picked up the drug. I mean I'd done relapse of the thought. So if I'd relapse of the thought, den dat's what I have to pay attention to more. It's my thinkin'. Den when I understand what the thinkin' is all about, den I know how to start controlin' my behavior. But when you been in the drug life and drinkin' and druggin' so long, every profession of people, anybody dat been in the drugs of life over thirty years, dey don't just quit like you supposed to quit, dey keep on relapsein', goin' back and back and relapse and back and back. Dey done been to a meetin' ten years ago and here it is another twenty years, dey still tryin' to figure out how to stop.

"It's just like, you know a hole right dere, you know a hole right dere in dat ground. It ain't small. It might look small but it ain't. See what I'm sayin'. Den when you not payin' attention, you walk right to it. You get close and you done fell right in dat hole. You relapse 'cause you ain't payin' attention. Dat hole is big, and you just wanna know how to go around it. But bein' into the drug life, drinkin' and druggin', it's always gonna be big.

"We see it different bein' addicts. We see it like, 'Oh, I can do just one.' Dat's the first thinkin' comin' outta my mind. 'I can only do one. I can only do one, or have dis one drink', but den when you sit down and do it, you see you can't have just one. Well you say, 'Shucks, I done fucked up again.' Den you say 'Man, I don't' know what to do.'

"Den you too much ashamed to go back to what you was doin'. And it ain't right, it don't feel right 'cause you done had a taste of clean and sober. And now you put more effort into tryin' to stay clean and sober. You gettin' to like dis new individual dat relapse was teachin' you, and den you go to dese meetin's and see all dese people dat have all dese means, and tellin' you to keep comin' back. But when you first get in the program you really don't understand what all dat mean 'cause you so tied up into your own thinkin', your own behavior.

"When you just into drinkin' and druggin', you don't know how to take a suggestion – advice. Den you sit dere and you wonder, 'Why don't I take dis advice the first time? Dey told me, dey told me, dey told me.' What happen? You done relapse. You don't want to face the truth dat someone told you dis suggestion.

"Even your parent, dey tell you, dey don't give you a suggestion, dey *tell* you – like your moms and dads say, 'Don't do dis. Don't hang with dat kid down the block. I know what he doin',' or 'Don't hang with dat girl. I know what she doin'.' But your own behavior, a action of your addiction 'cause you to go an do it anyway. You wanna go in dere and see what you can learn. You wanna taste to see what it's like. But den when you taste it, you done relapsed, den you go right back and say, 'I done did dat. I done did dat again.'

"Just like a gambler, like any kind'a addiction: a check writer, a liar, a molester... You know what I'm sayin'? Any type a person like dat, dey have an addiction problem, and dey don't really face it, but when dey face it, dey go to dese meetin's. Dey know dey have a problem. But a kid, dey don't want to take the relapse responsibility of doin' what's right. You see what I'm sayin'?

"'Cause relapse is like when you a child. When you first born in dis world, you fall down, and you get right back up. When you a first born baby, you ain't gonna just stay down dere, you gonna get up! But if you don't wanna get up, den someone always gonna come along and help you. Dats what a treatment program is. Dey gonna keep lovin' you until you learn to love yourself. Dat's what recoverin' is about. Goin' to meetin's, gettin' to know the twelve steps and gettin' to understand what peoples is all about, especially me, myself. And myself is the biggest problem dat it is, beatin' up myself, especially when you done relapsed already.

"Some people, dey go out and dey can't come back 'cause dey done relapsed. Dey be so tied up into deir life. Deir pride come in front of dem or deir jealousy or deir shame. Dey know dey done relapsed, but how dey gonna make it?

"Dere's only one way dey know; deir behavior kick back in to sell drugs and use drugs, drinkin', women, prostitution, all dis kick back into deir street life. 'Cause when you start drinkin' and druggin', when you really get a taste of a drug life, you learn how to lie to the po-lice. You learn how to lie to your mom, your dad. You learn to run from people, run from the po-lice, run from everybody. Dat's what your addiction do to ya. Sometime it tell you, face yourself, and sometime when you into dat type of world, you run from you. What I mean you run from you? You run from bein' responsible who you are. You see what I'm sayin'?

"Den you wanna know, 'Wow, who am I?' But you really don't know who you is 'cause you been drinkin' and druggin' so long dat you only know the person dat who doin' the drugs, but you don't know the real person dat inside of you, the nice person, the lovin' person. Or you just have the bad behavior of drinkin' and druggin', and you don't want to let nobody in. Everyone done try to help you, but you don't look at how many bridges of drinkin' and druggin' dat you done burned.

"See, when I been drinkin' and druggin', I done burnt alotta bridges, and I still had dat behavior today. When I relapse back in the days, I still burn some bridges. In your heart the program teach you how to fix it, but when it still does come to you, you can't fix it right now, you might have to just put it on the side and let it go. You know what I'm sayin'?

"When you sober, den you wanna realize, can you do it? Dat's when fightin' for recovery come in dere. You wanna stay clean. You wanna see, can you try to stay clean? And deep inside of you you do want dat, but dis behavior of relapse keep tellin' you, 'I can't, I can't.' You did dis and did dat in your drinkin' and druggin' days, but you maybe can't do it when you sober.

"But dere ain't no such thing, I can't. Ain't no such thing in the world dat I can't. You can do it, but you gotta be able to have dat ability ta see. What I mean see, you got eyes, you can see, but deep inside your mind you are really blind. It's just like your thinkin'. You can see what goin' on in your thinkin' of your drinkin' and druggin' days.

(I'm not sure where Willie gets his "can do" attitude. Some of it might be from AA, though from what I've read, they mostly talk about being able to make it clean and sober with the help of "your higher power."

I think it is just part of who Willie is, part of why people are attracted to him. He has a lot of gumption, and he doesn't let anyone tell him what he can or can't do, in fact, he sees that as a challenge.)

"But the biggest problem with the person bein' clean and sober is dat you gotta have alotta other activities. You gotta find new toys to help you deal with it. 'Cause if you don't find other new toys to deal with it, some way dat relapse startin' to kick in real strong.

"How my momma say, 'The idle mind is the devil playground.' Dat's the truth. And dat's the way addiction is. Addiction can go to sleep for many, many, many years, but it never sleep. You try to forget about it, but it still pop back up once in a while.

"Alotta people know Bill W. who wrote the AA book. He was an alcoholic, but he still fought to make the decision in dat book to change. He had dat decision before he start writin' the book, he wanted to stop drinkin' and druggin'. He took prescription pills. He was an addict.

"I don't want people to think dat I don't know recovery 'cause I'm an addict. I'm doin' just what any other addicts do, tryin' to change my life, tryin' to better my life, tryin' to find the true person dat my parents brought me into dis world to be, but I done got so caught up in drinkin' and druggin' like my whole generation. All I ever know was drinkin' and druggin', so quite naturally I got into part of dat.

"It's a behavior dat each human bein' have. We relapse on somethin' 'cause we got a drug addiction. We wanna make ourself like a human bein' and feel good. Everyone wanna feel good in dis world.

"See, alotta people get into a rehab program where dey get it the first time. Yeah, some peoples do first time get it 'cause dey was deep into it and dey was tired. Dey was tired of drinkin' and druggin'.

"But a person, a person dat really like it like I have... I liked it. It made me feel good. I was abusive to womens, and abusive to some other people. I done robb'ded people.

"Lotta people say dat relapse ain't part of recovery, but I believe it is part of recovery.

"But me. I was in the streets so long. I was in the streets for over thirty years. Runnin' up and down in the rain. As bad as I wanna stop gettin' high, my thinkin' and my body was tellin' me, my body achin', I couldn't stop. I did get arrested. My relapse still say, 'I can have one. I can have one.' Just like when I was a kid. I never stop smokin' marijuana. I love marijuana. When I got older I had to stop smokin' marijuana 'cause I was on probation.

"In Wisconsin dey give you alotta drug tests. Dat's when I start substitute one drug for another drug – drinkin' for drugs. Coke only last seventy-two hours. Not really seventy-two hours. It depends on how much you do. It stays in longer den you expect it. I went to drinkin', smokin' coke again, snortin' coke.

"I relapse. I constantly, constantly relapse. I can't never figure out how to stop relapsin' until I keep going to dese meetin's to figure it out. I didn't even work. I couldn't go to work 'cause I was gettin' high. Dat's what relapsin' is, is tryin' to learn how to stop relapsin'; to see a true picture of what relapsin' is.

"It's a disease. You have to pay attention so you don't relapse. If you don't, you will relapse. Any addict dat go to the meetin's, dey know what I'm talkin' about."

"So how do you know when you figured it out? I mean, you heard it lots of times, the same stuff over and over about how to stay sober."

"You keep goin' to ta meetin's, dats how. Like Friday. I had a hard time Friday. My check was eight hundred some dollars, and dey took out three hundred some dollars for taxes. I was pissed. Angry. Den I go to the bank and get out

The relapsin' already happen and I know it. I done relapsed. I hadn't put in the process yet but I'm thinkin' 'bout it. I'm mopin' around the house, turnin' my music up, dis and dat. I be waitin' on my roommate.

"Den he say, 'Can she get me some, too?'

"'Sure she can get you some, too.'

"Den my recovery thinkin' comin' back in while I'm livin' it, and I say, 'I don't wanna fuck dat up. I'm livin' in a clean and sober place, I don't wanna mess dat up.'

"I tell my roommate, 'Oh, dat's okay.'

"I'm usin' my recovery tools and my relapse tools at the same time. So I get one of my roommates. I tell him to take me to the movie. He didn't feel like goin'.

"I told him, 'Dis is part of recovery. I feel like usin'. I wanna do somethin' to help myself.' So I tell somebody about my relapse and my recovery for the first time

"'All right, I'll take you to the movie, and you call me when you get out.'

"I say, 'Okay.'

"So we get dressed. We go to the theater Friday. The movie don't start until an hour and a half. He tell me I can go in dere and sit down. I ain't gonna do dat. I say 'Take me home,' but I didn't really go home. What I did, I took him to a video store to buy some movies. From dere we went to Walgreen to buy some foot powder, den I came home. I'm tired already. I already worked a whole week. And I know I have to be at work tomorrow at seven. I have to get up at five thirty. I already know dis.

"I seen my relapsin' behavior, so what I did, I learn how to recognize it. I ain't sayin' it was controlled, all I say is I recognized my relapsin'.

"Most of the person who been drinkin' and druggin', dey can't go a day, if dey really, really out dere really bad, dey can't go a day without usin'. Somethin' in deir mind tell dem, 'I ain't gonna drink for dis time of the month.' Dat don't' mean it ain't gonna happen. You might not drink dis moment, you have good intention, but at dat moment your thinkin' change again. 'Cause it's dat relapse behavior dat you have with drinkin' and druggin'.

"I did everythin' I could Friday to stay clean and sober, like today. I don't feel like usin' at all today.

"Saturday I took it easy. I went to work. I got off yesterday at two thirty. I could have been still workin'. I didn't have my driver's license. My boss say if I done had my drivers license, I could have still been workin'. See dat relapse come in again yesterday. Dat relapse kick on more and more every time you think you got it right, you ain't got it right, but you done relapsed again, already. I did it Friday, I did it Saturday. Today I haven't done it, 'cause I'm sittin' around and watchin' TV.

"Saturday I get off work at two thirty. sometimes a person like me, when you know you got alotta money in the bank, dat relapse come tell you, go ahead and spend it. You don't really think about messin' it up on drinkin' and druggin' and womens. And you say, forget it.

"Show you how a relpase work. On my way home Saturday, I was walkin' home. I see a guy I know in a van. I know he ain't up to no good. And he had a girl in the van with 'em. All I had to do is open my own mouth and say let's go. Dey would'a jumped to it. Dey had two demons already inside dem waitin' to get high. Dey ain't gonna spend deir money on it. Dey gonna use my money and party with me, den I would'a have to pay for three parties all at once.

"My relapse would'a kicked in and say, 'Lets get some coke and get some beer.' Den it would'a started from dere.

"The girl, I knew her. I already had sex with her before. She was a nice girl, but I looked at her. I decided I didn't need her no more at dat time, but the demon of relapse told me I did need her.

"I just looked at her hard, and I just keep my mouth closed, 'cause my relapse kickin' in. It was hurtin'me, too, while I was in the van gettin' a ride home. It was beatin' me up."

"So you went in the van with these people?" *I can't believe he did that to himself, put himself in that situation; Like he was trying to tempt fate.*

"I got in the van. So when I got in the van and I seen 'em, den all dese demons and the spirits dat was inside'a relapse of drinkin' and druggin', it was dere. I know dey was drinkin' beer already. So as it happened, I controlled myself at dat time, but I already had relapse with my thinkin'. It already happened at the job way before den.

"See dat's how you startin' to recognize the relapse of things dat you doin' when you ain't payin' attention to it. Dat's how you fall back into dat hole.

"See, I already got a taste of clean and sober. I already had it once before, a taste of it. It was a wonderful thing. But the biggest problem bein' clean and sober is you gotta find somethin' to do with your time. You gotta find a young lady, even though you maybe don't trust 'em. You still gotta find one a little decent. If you don't find one a little decent, and you let your life and your thinkin' get back in the way, den you gonna relapse. Especially when a male and female like sex and dey wanna fill deir need. I don't know about womens, but guys same as womens when dey been around so many girls. Dey wanna solve deir problem, deir problem of wantin' to be with someone. And dat's how relapse attack individuals like us sometime, when we get lonely. Dat how the program – intervention – teachin' us how to talk to people, askin' a favor. Den you take up dem tools you learned in rehab, and you turn it around on a sober basis. Dat's how you work with stuff like dat.

"It's difficult bein' sober, it really is. I ain't sayin' it's a bad thing, but it's a terrible thing for someone like me who been drinkin' an druggin' for a long time. And you know I ain't never been shy about talkin' to no womens or mens. I ain't never been shy about dat. Dat was a gift God gave me way before drinkin' and druggin', but when I'm drinkin' and druggin', I think I'm more slicker. Dat's the issue on dat."

"So do you know how many times you've been sober?"

"Prob'bly three times. Dis is the fourth dat I'm gettin' the chance. I can count 'em. Only time I know I stay sober is when I go to prison. I don't count dat. I'm talkin' 'bout being out on the streets and bein' sober."

"So you can't get any drugs when you're in prison?"

"Yeah, you can get anythin' you want in prison."

"So why do you stay sober in prison?"

"'Cause in prison when you sober you have a functionin' mind, but when you not sober, you don't. When you sober you have a sober mind and you know what's goin' on, but when you ain't sober in prison, you always get into alotta easy bad trouble. Den you get in debt, and debts not nice to have in prison.

"You gonna pay one way or another. I'll tell you straight out. You gonna pay the money or you gonna pay your ass. Either one of dem you gonna pay. You do get paid once a month bein' in prison."

"You get an allotment of money?"

"No, you work for like thirty cent an hour, maybe lesser den dat."

"Whatever job you do?"

"Right, whatever job. Or if you be goin' to school you get like, in Chicago it's like fifteen dollars, but in Wisconsin you get like seven or eight dollars, so you lose. Den if you owe somebody, dats how dey get deir money. And if you ain't got enough, you really in trouble. Depends on how big your debt is. Dat's the reason I didn't get high. I tried to get high once in Chicago. I was in Danville, Illinois prison, and my roomate is a Latin King. He had alotta money. He had cups (a cup is a cap off a pop or beer bottle that's used to measure drugs), a wrapped cup, it be worth sixty to seventy dollars. And people dat have dat much cash had alotta juice – pull with the cops. Dey know people.

"If you get a cup and you can't pay it back, you be in trouble, not a little trouble, I'm talkin' 'bout really big trouble. You gonna get extortion. One way or another you gonna be deir bitch.

"When I tried to get high in dere, we smoked a joint. A joint was really, really, really fine, like a little tooth pick. And dey put a little weed in it. And dat costed three dollars. We tried to watch the Bulls playoff; you know, when the Bulls won. And I didn't like feelin' exposed, like hyper-phobic. I didn't like dat 'cause I couldn't move around. I couldn't do none a dat, so dat's the first time I did dat, and I didn't never get high again. So dat's the reason why."

"All the different recovery programs you've been in, are they all the twelve steps?"

"Dey all the twelve step, but dey different names of recovery. You got NA [Narcotics Anonymous], Twelve

Traditional, AA [Alcoholics Anonymous], all the different kinds.

Dey all say everybody is an addict. Whatever your desire is, if you can control it, dat's ok, but you can't really control it 'cause your thinkin' have you desire it. It's just like good and evil. We all got thinkin' in our life dat we want to explore, just like a wild animal. He go out dere where he don't wanna be, but he still wanna explore. He go around his territory dat he know, dat he comfortable with. He still wanna see what's goin' on."

Then Willie falls off the end of the earth.

CHAPTER 11

Relapse Number Two

~~~

April 15, 2011, 3:47pm (phone message)

Hey sister. Hope you doin' okay. I'm doin' okay. I done relapsed. Somethin' trigger me off, and I go out and use. So I'll talk with you later. Bye

April 21st, 2011 (On the phone with Willie.)
"Hey Willie. How you doin'?"
"Not so good. I'm hurtin,' hurtin' real bad."
"I suppose. You were doing so good. What happened?"
"I relapsed?"
"I know."
"How long were you out for?"
"Three days. Now I'm just lickin' my wounds."

(It's déjà vu. Those same words came out of that same mouth after the last time he had relapsed. The last time it was with the girl he wanted to stay with. I remember the day. I had driven my motorcycle to work, and I stopped at a gas station on my way home to fill up. I hadn't heard from Willie in a couple weeks, so when I got his message, I called him back right away.)

"Have you started back to school yet?" I ask.

"No."

"Well maybe next week."

"How's your book goin'?" (Willie's referring to another book I am working on, not the one with him.)

"It's going good."

"You gonna make a millgion dollars?"

"I don't know about that."

"Yeah, when you make it, you will."

(He has more confidence than me!)

"I've been working on your book."

"Yeah?" (His voice finally perks up – more like he usually sounds. This is heart-warming to me, but I think, *But are you going to be around to finish this with me?*)

"How many chapters you got?"

"I think about seven, maybe more."

"Is it gonna be a long book or a short one?"

"Not really long. But we're not done yet. We have more to talk about. Are you able to meet next week to talk?" (I'm hoping if talking about his book perked him up today, maybe it would give him something to look forward to.)

"I don't know. I'll have to call ya."
(I guess not that much.)
"All right."
"You take care, Willie."
"Okay."
"Bye."
"Bye."

I go to the Oxford House again to meet with Willie. He wants to talk about love. Before we started the conversation, Willie suggested we sit in a room where his roommates aren't sitting. I want to find out about his recent relapse, while it's fresh in his mind.

I find out later, he doesn't want them to hear about his relapse. It's against the rules, of course. If you are living in this house, you can't use. And Willie is one of the people in charge in the house, so it would look even worse for him. Willie went on a short bender, and he's not proud of it.

We start out with a little light conversation.

"Was your mom a very good cook?"
"Yeah, yeah. She cook her ass off.
"I talked to her Sunday or Saturday. No, I think dat was Friday. She's doin' fine"
"How often do you talk to your mom?"
"Shit. I don't know. Last year I talked to her a lot, but dis year I talked to her once. She got her phone turned off den. When my brother went to jail, dat's how her phone

got chopped off. He callin' collect. So dat went through the roof. I called my cousin and he called her. Den he had to call another cousin to get through. And when I got through, she glad to hear from me. She say she want me to come dere for Thanksgivin'."

"Well, that'd be good."

"I'm thinkin' about it."

"That'd be okay to go see your mom?"

"I have to ax the mother fucker... I gotta ax... my PO."

"Excuse your French."

"You done say dat. I ain't gonna say dat. I have to ax permission to see my real mother dat birthed me."

"So you have to stay in the area for your probation?"

"I can go anywhere, I just have to ax before I go."

"Oh, okay."

"If I don't, it's like a state. Since I'm doin so good, I don't have no problem with dat mother fucker. I'll ax. It ain't gonna hurt."

"Is this the same guy that ... "

"Locked me up? Yeah. If I fuck up if he would get the twelve and a half years, he'd get me more than two and a half. Dat's what I'm thinkin'.

(Willie explains to me that after his first conviction for robbery in Wisconsin in 2007, he could have gotten twelve and a half years probation - that was the maximum sentence. What he got was a year in jail and five years probation, two and a half of which he had already served. I would guess the conviction was so severe because of all the other convictions that he had in Illinois before this robbery conviction in Wisconsin – twenty three to be exact – plus the nine additional he had acquired here before that robbery conviction.)

"Can we talk about when you relapsed a couple weeks ago?"

"As I seen you dat day, dat Thursday night, dat loneliness kicked in. I did everythin' in my power to avoid it. I even called people at the meetin'. Dey say dey ain't got time, dis and dat, and I didn't feel like ridin' my bike, so I call Roxanne. Dat's a night girl. So I call her and I ax her how she doin'. She say she doin' okay.

"Den I say, 'What's goin' on?'

"Den she say, 'What you need, daddy.'

"'Well, I need a piece a dat pie.'

"'How much you got?'

"I got a few dollars.

"She say, 'If you got fifty, I can shake your tree and give you a piece a pie.'

"I say, 'Okay.'

"So I get on my bike, and I'm headin' dat way, and I changed my mind. I know she was drinkin' and dis and dat, so I change my mind. I went to a shorter detour around here about Darbo and East Washington. It was around eight at night. I went over to a friend's house, and he had like three girls dere.

"I tell'em, I say, 'What's up, man.'

"And he say, 'Not much'

"I say, 'Which one can give me a piece a dat pie?'

"All dem girls say, 'I will, I will, I will.' You know what I'm sayin'?

"Den dey say, 'Fifty dollars.'

"I say, 'Okay.'

"So I give her twenty-five first. All right.

"Den she play with shot gun, I call duke.

"Is this that guy...?"

"No, dat's me. My penis duke."

Really? Do all guys give their penis' a name? I could ask my husband but I'm not sure he'd appreciate the question.

"So did you really say, who's gonna give me a piece of pie. Is that like...?"

"Dat's a women's vigina. Dat's a good thing. Dat' instead of comin' out and sayin' come on girl give me...? you know."

"Yeah."

"And she understands that lingo?"

"Dat's street slang. Dat's easy sayin' instead'a sayin', hoe you gonna give me some of dis and dat... and she know what dat is."

"Is that in Chicago and Madison?"

"No, I just whipped dat up, like a nickname. Dat's my nickname. So dey know me. Dey know me so dey except it as dat.

"And dey say, okay, and I give half: twenty-five.

"We go in the basement. She done licked on duke for a while.

"Den she say, 'I wanna get me somethin.'

"'Oh girl, I'm tryin' ta do right.'

"'No, he just be here right in five minutes.'

"I end up given her the whole fifty without gettin' dat pie first. So she got her stuff, and she's sittin' in front of me smokin'. She tease me when she took her hit.

"'All right. Let me blow some smoke on duke.' She wanna suck it and at the same time she smokin'.

"And I say, 'Okay.' And dat brought back a memory.

"Den I turn around and say, 'Fuck it. Let's go all the way.'

"So I went all the way. [He smoked the drug with her]. Den I went and got some money outta the bank. I got five hundred dollars. My savings."

"So you had to leave the house where the woman is at?"

"Right, I had to leave and go to the Tyme machine and get money out the bank."

"So why'd you...?"

"Why'd I leave?"

"No, why'd you start all this? What was going on that made you..."

"Wanna do dat?"

"When you into the world like I am, you can not get lonely. You foolin' yourself. You want some love companion, somebody to hang out with, to talk with, to love or maybe just out to a movie with 'em. Just show 'em you appreciate you love or you like 'em.

"With addicts, dat's our biggest problem is loneliness. If we don't fix nothin' in our life and keep busy, our mind starts to wonderin' how it used to be. Den we start thinkin', we say, 'Well, what I'm gonna do?' Den you gotta find somethin' to do. If you don't and you let it stay dere for a minute or two, you start thinkin' of your old behavior. Your old behavior start flashin' up and you have a pretty picture. But you done forget the bad things in your life dat put you in dat situation.

"Den you try and try to fight it. It maybe go away for a few seconds, but den somehow it jump right back on 'cause you still in dis environment. You still lonely. You see what I'm sayin'?

"Dat's why people like me get high, so we won't be lonely. So we cover up dat fake love, and dey ain't got nobody dat comfort dem.

"Dat's our biggest problem. We get into drinkin' and druggin' 'cause we lonely, we wanna hang out, we want somebody to love us. Even though we prob'bly got somebody to love us, but we ain't payin' attention to it 'cause we don't really see it, and we don't hear it.

"So dat's how it happened. Dat's why last time we talked about relapse. Dat's a relapse. Before you relapse, you done relapse way, way, way back prob'bly four months ago before you thought about it. Den when you thought about it, you fightin' it, you fightin' it. When it do come to you, it hits you. Well, I gotta go get a piece a pie. Den you move on from dere.

"And you feel in your heart dat dat's love, but you know it's not love, it's pain. And you like dat pain and dat drama dat you goin' through in bein' an addict and an alcoholic.

"Dats why people go to bars 'cause dey sit dere, dey want somebody to love 'em, to talk bullshit to 'em. Dey know it's bullshit, but dey want dat love and comfort, companionship. Dey say, 'Hey, it's ok.'

"Dat ain't ok. You know what I'm sayin'?

"But what I get at dis house is a cock blocker; someone here to block you from doin' what you want. All the time you have to feed him, feed him, feed him drugs, before you get to your destination [what Willie was looking for – in this case, sex]. Dat's chaos."

"Did you say cock blocker?"

"Dat means you tryin' to get some piece a pie. In dese smoke houses dere's alotta peoples in dere. You don't really have to give 'em none of your drugs you just suppose to give the people, whosever house it is, you give *dem* some. You give some from what you buy; you show 'em appreciation. Dis what I'm given you to be in your house, to sit in your house and dis and dat. If I smoke, you smoke."

(Drug etiquette 101.)

"So when you went to the bank you had to get money..."

"Not only for myself but for all the other cock blockers dat wanna sit around and get high. Dey don't want to go out and hustle. So what you gotta do, you gotta prob'bly spend like a hundred dollars. Den after you get through smokin', now you ready for the piece of pie for real.

"Now you just tell the house person, 'Look here, I'd like to hollar at you.'

"Dey say, 'What's up?'

"'I wanna give you dis so and so for a room and take dis young lady in dere... You know what I wanna do.'

"Dey say, 'Sure.'

"Dey charge you for the room. So you ask whether dey want dope or money. You have to give 'em dat so dey won't bother you so you can do what you wanna do."

"So do these women live at this place or do they just work there?"

"Dey homeless and dey street walkers. Dey street walkers, somebody who like to get high and know her body can get alotta things for her. And so she use her body to get her addiction done. Even though she don't want to, but she do it 'cause she wanna feel good. And if the guy treatin' her right, she gonna feel good. Dat's how you be able to have it in a house. Dey's always gonna be a women dere like dat, sittin' around, gettin' high. She nice lookin'. But once you start smokin' and drinkin', she really nice lookin'!" (Willie laughs.)

"You knew this house?"

"I knew dis house from the past. I been dere before. I didn't feel like goin' farther. As it happened I went dere, and I stayed out for a day and a half."

"Did you miss work? Were you supposed to be working?"

"I had two days off. Dat was the hurtin' part. You gotta fill dat void. The relapse came and caught you. And your mind start thinkin', 'How you gonna fix it?' Dat's when you go out into dis world and be caught up.

"Any person who drink and do drugs, an alcoholic, dey have dis addiction dat never leave, it only sleep. And when it do hit you, it hit you hard. Dat's how relapse come.

"Or you been into dat environment, addicted to dat environment. You may not use, but you into dat same behavior with dese people who are doin' it. You may be sellin' drugs, or usin', or doin' somethin' dat illegal in dat type of environment with dem. So you sit dere and you don't know how to get out.

"It's just like a drug dealer. He wanna sell you dope 'cause he addicted to doin' dat. He addicted to dat money, he addicted to the car. He the same as me.

Dey smoke alotta marijuana and dey drinks. And some don't drink, but dey addicted to dat environment, same as me. Same as I'm addicted to does women at night. I think about 'em all the time.

"We all have dis addiction dat part of our life. We

wanna be happy. So when we don't be happy all the time, we try to find the void dat inside to fill it up. We know it's an empty void dere, but we don't tell everybody the empty void dere, we just keep it in our mind and our mind just drill on it. Say, 'When it gonna happen, when it gonna happen?' We know relapse gonna happen.

"Some people got sex addiction, like a child molester. Dey have dis thinkin' just everybody have, dat behavior. Dey wanna stop what dey doin', but dey so tied up into dat environment, deir behavior, dey can't.

"Den when dey go get a taste a doin' the right thing, den dat relapse start kickin' in harder. Den dey wanna learn to stop relapsin', but it constantly keep comin'. It's dere constantly.

"From twenty or thirty years down the line, dat behavior still pop up. Like some people in AA, NA, dey be clean for twenty, thirty years and dey go out and relapse.

"How do dey relapse? Stop goin' to meetin's, stop hangin' out with the same people who was clean like dem. Den dey start tryin' to show off, go back to the old neighborhood. Dey say, 'Look how I'm lookin' good."

"But you can't do dat. Once you change your mind, you gotta stay with people dat positive. Stay with people dat clean. Like dey say, birds of a feather stick together. Dat is true. Because you know what you gonna stick with, what you like, what make you feel good, even if it's drama. Even if it's a bad behavior, you gonna know dose type'a people. Dat's what addiction is. Dat's how people get out and go relapse.

"You said you were out for three days?"

"Two day and a half."

"What made you go home? Did you stay at this house that whole time?"

"Yeah. What made me come home was I was tired, and my thinkin' startin' to catch up with me. I thought about the money dat I lost. I thought how I had to start all over again. I was angry, mad, disappointed, upset. And what make it so bad was I was doin' so good. Matter-a-fact, your brother tease'ded me dat day.

"He say, 'Well, Willie, I'm surprised you doin' good.'

"'Earl, I cannot pat myself on the back right now, 'cause I'm scared.'

"He say, 'What if I dropped you off on Darbo and East Washington?'

"I say, 'I can't make it.'"

"Is that a bad place?"

"Yeah, dats a bad place where I usually go and hang out and get caught up. I'm know over dere real good, and it's easy for me to hustle like in Chicago. I can go to a certain area and just get one – a bag of drugs, whatever drug you want. And I find somehow, madness come to me. But if you ain't got no dope or money, the womens move onto the next individual and give 'em the piece a pie. Dat's what dey do to survive. You really can't get mad at her for what she doin'. She only doin' to support her habit. Same as what you doin' to support your habit."

"So how much money did you lose?"

"Be honest, I lost about nine hundred dollars. Nine hundred."

"I'd like nine hundred dollars, Willie."

"I would, too, but you know dat's part of relapsin'. Because when you relapsin', you don't think of the money. Money ain't a value no more. What a value is how to make yourself feel good. How you enjoyin' dis bad chaos and behavior.

"Den you wonder how you gonna get it back, your money back to pay your bills, to buy things you want, to go to movies. Dat's if a person got a job. If a person ain't got a job, he out dere on the streets homeless, he wouldn't care. First of all, he prob'bly stole it or he prob'bly hustle it, or he prob'bly trick somebody out of it. But a workin' person, it's a different story. When dey work to get all dis hard money, den dey turn around and give it away, dey get upset about it.

"But every time it come down to the point, was you happy? Dat's the first thing alotta people ax you: Was you happy? Did it make you feel good? Yes, it *did* make me feel good. Still you had chaos right dere, and you angry about dat.

"Bein' an addict and a workin' individual, you think you function in dis behavior 'cause you work every day, but you don't. Your life is unmanageable: your mind, your thinkin', your eyesight, your love. It's just a illusion dat it's managable. And you know it's not managable. But you just go along with the program 'cause dats the behavior of addiction.

"When you see dat addiction, den you wanna know why it happen to you. You no different den the next individual dat have dat behavior. Dey wanna stop, but dey can't.

"Just like people who go shoppin'. It's a behavior, it's a disease. First thing dey say is, 'I ain't goin' shoppin' dis day,' and dey relapse and dey go shoppin'. Same as some people, dey steal. Dey can't help themselves, pickin' up somethin' out the store dat don't belong to dem. It's a behavior. Den dey done relapse, too.

"You always relapse before you do the crime or before you do whatever you do. Your mind visual it, how it's gonna be. But it's the same.

"Only a suggestion dat I can give, is dat people read the big book: AA, NA book. Dats good. Or a church can help you, or you just find a way to keep yourself busy from dat thinkin'. Den you gotta find true love. Another true love. You think you love drinkin' and druggin', but you really don't love dat 'cause you don't' know. You know what I'm sayin'?"

"Something to do that you enjoy, you mean?"

"Right.

"Once you get to like somethin' for so long, you start lovin' it. You love what you do. Like me. I like to fool with different womens. Even though I might not get what I want from her, it's just a gift I like to do. I say, 'Can I do it?' Just to see, can I be with her.

"And dat's a behavior you have bein' a human bein. You think, can I do it? Den when you see you can, den dats when your addiction kick in, and dat's what made you feel good. Dat's what it's all about."

"So what made you come back?"

"My home. Things I done lost so many times in my life dat I'm tired of losin'.

"See, you get a taste of clean and sober, you get tired of losin'. You know dats a losin' battle. You know it. Anybody dat got an addiction problem, drinkin' and druggin' or any habit, dey know it's a bad losin' battle.

"Den you lose. Den you say, 'Man, I'm losin' again.' I lost dis and I lost dat. If you ain't got none'a dem things to hold onto, to fight for, you don't care.

Dat means when you out dere in the streets and you lettin' it go, like when I was homeless in Chicago, you don't care. I didn't care if I lost nothin' or gained nothin' 'cause I know in my mind I can get it back.

"Now when you go in dese programs, you have a choice. Do you wanna keep dis what you have or you just wanna throw it away?

"When you get somethin', settle down, you get a nice place to stay and dis and dat, you start feelin' comfortable. Den you don't wanna make no stupid, foolish mistake. But dat relapse inside'a you, you know it gonna happen. But you gotta find a way so it won't happen. You see what I'm sayin'?"

"I'm glad you came back, Willie"

"I am glad myself. It's a little better now. I got sa'more money saved up. About a thousand dollars. But I got it different dis time."

"What do you mean?"

"I got my job savin' it. I got my job takin' care'a the money. Dey keep it at the job. I use the bank for another tool 'till I learn how to control my behavior. I know I gotta learn how to see it before it happen. Den once I see it happen, den I have a choice to do dis or not to do dis. Dats what I'm learnin' now. And to be good.

"Lotta people tell you when you be an addict, 'Be good!' And you say, 'Be good, too.' So you start and let dat rub on you, to be good, so you can pay more attention to what you doin'."

"How do you think you could have avoided what happened a couple weeks ago?"

"I really couldn't.
"I could have waited 'till the next day and went straight

to sleep. But I should have forced myself to do somethin' or let someone else to help me, or just went to bed.

"When you relapse all dese things start comin' to you now. You wanna know how you gonna think a different way to change dis situation again. Dat's what part of relapse is to me. You learnin' how to think and make a better thinkin' of yourself, and a better choice so you can deal with a problem. 'Cause you know it's a problem, and it always gonna be dere for you 'cause you's an addict. So you have to make up some other better way to doin' it."

"Do you think there would somebody else you can call?"

(I really do want Willie to succeed at this, so I am trying to think of other options for Willie when he feels like using.)

"Well, you can call people at AA and NA in Madison. But one thing I notice about peoples in Madison in the program. See, dey talk all dis good talk, but when you really, really need someone to come over, dey don't get up and go. Dey say dey try, dis and dat over the phone, but when you say, 'Hey, man, let's go hang out.' Dey tell you a thousand excuses.

"I ain't sayin' all dem be dat way, but the ones I been seein', been my sponsor, dey got other things to do.

"You gotta fire dat guy dat be your sponsor 'till you find someone comfortable in your skin. Tell you start realizin' how to deal with dat problem. Den when you understand dat dat's a problem, den you have someone to call all the time.

"When people don't want to be bothered, dey don't answer deir phone, dey don't wanna do dis, dey don't wanna get up. Dey tell you all dese lies. Dey say, 'I got somethin' ta do.'"

"Can you still call. . . ? I can't remember their names. There are two men at different churches, that you know, right?"

"I can call Paul and Will. But sometimes dey kind'a get busy, too. Dey got other things in life.

"What come right back to it is dat you gotta put your faith in God. You gotta turn around and put your thinkin', what dey say in the program, who ever your God can be dat helps you with dis situation.

"But deep inside, I believe in God who created all, everythin', heaven and earth. Dat's the God I believe in. I have to put my faith more in him. He say he sent his son, Jesus Christ, to die on the cross for me, so I have to put my faith in God, den have Jesus to work the miracles with me. But I have to put some work in myself, too."

"That's easy to say."

"Yes it is."

"But when you were there. . . you know, Thursday night; where was God then?"

"Ya know, he was dere. He payin' attention. He be dere in your thinkin'. Dat how the other thinkin', the better thinkin' come in to conquer what you be thinkin' of doin', with the drugs. He make you think of it before you do it.

"You think of two choices, the right choice and the wrong choice. The good choice, He tell you once, den He'll stand back and let you make a decision and see what decision you gonna make. Even though He know you gonna make the wrong decision, He'll still stand by you and come back to you to help you. But the old thinkin' don't do dat. The old behavior, the bad side, just don't care.

"Dat's how dat go."

(I guess I have to agree with him on this one.)

CHAPTER 12

DECEMBER 6, 2010

~~~~~~

I am meeting Willie for lunch. He wants to treat. He received a gift card for Christmas, so he wants to take me out for lunch. I pick him up at Chris's auto body. He says Chris "doesn't do shit." He says he's already made his "wad" of money so he doesn't need to do anything. Willie says Chris would rather be doing something else.

Willie gives me a brotherly hug.

We go to Panera. On the way there he's flirting again.

"I'm waiting for you to call me sister," I say.
"I'm gettin' dere, but I ain't dere yet," he says.
"I hope you get there pretty soon."
"I'm startin' to get the idea," he adds.

He talks about how he and my brother Earl are friends, how it took Earl a while to be his friend. He likes my mother. He calls her "your Old Girl".

He asks me, "How come when you married, you didn't stay married?"

"It just didn't work out," I reply, not really feeling like getting into the heavy topic.

"My grandmother, she had twenty-two kids with the same guy, and dey stayed together. I'm like dat," he says with confidence, even though he has never been married.

"Twenty-two kids? Really?"

"Yeah, twenty-two."

(I'm not sure I believe him on this. I think he believes it was twenty-two, but I don't think a woman can have that many children and not have her uterus fall out after number fifteen or so.)

"If you don't stay married, you not my sister anymore," he says with a sly grin and a laugh.

"Your Old Girl stayed with her husband. You like your Old Girl."

"I suppose," I say.

"I like your Aunt Kay. You know I call her cupcake? Your mom like'ded dat. Kay said she'd buy me boots if I tied my boots. I did dat for six months and when she didn't buy me the boots, I stopped tyin' 'em. I started tyin' 'em again, and she finally bought me the boots. Now I just tie 'em when I see her. Dey were really cheap boots, so I gave 'em away."

Willie tells me he started back to school this last Monday: math and English.

"Den once I build dat grade up, I can go onto carpentry. I'm doin' school through March," he explained.

"How do you like English?"

"I like math. I was good in math in high school. I need to get back into it. It's hard goin' back after bein' away."

Willie talks very little about women today, which is good. He needs to concentrate on other things.

"You know I'm goin' to New Orlins."

"I heard about that from Earl. When are you going?"

"End of December or January."

"That ought to be fun. Are you going with Dave's church?"

"Yeah. Ten or fifteen of us is goin'. We gonna work on fixin' up a house. The church set up somethin' so we can go in dere."

Willie tells me he needs a sleeping bag for the trip. I'll let him use one of ours and hope I get it back. We have extra in case it doesn't make it home again. He also asks for some venison from my husband. Willie has had venison before, and he knows my husband hunts, so he decides that maybe we can supply him with some.

I drop him back off at the bodyshop where he's working or hanging out, I can't really tell, and not a minute later he calls me on my cell phone.

"What's up, sis? You like dat. I was just practicin' dat sister thing."

I'm supposed to call him brother. So I call him bro.

Maybe I can relax a little now that he's not constantly trying to scam on me. A little, anyway.

Sat Feb 5th, 2011 (a cell phone call).

"Hey Sister, what's up, man. I'm back from New Orlins. I was callin' just to let you know I'm back. I ran out of money to buy you a present from New Olrins. I sorry 'bout dat. I hope you have a nice day. I talked to your Old Girl and your brother. Ain't nobody else to call, so be good, sister. I'll catch you later. Bye."

CHAPTER 13
Serious Time

~~~~~~~

I don't hear from Willie for over a week, which is a bit unusual for him. After week two rolls by without hearing from him, I give my brother a call.

"Have you heard from Willie lately?"

"Nope. He's probably in jail."

"Well, if you hear from him, tell him I need to get that audio book back to the library."

(I had taken the audio book *Angela's Ashes* out of the library for Willie to listen to because I knew he didn't like to read. I think reading is too much work for him, so he just doesn't bother.)

"You can kiss that goodbye," my brother crows. "You ain't gettin' that back."

(I know he might be right about that, but I also know Willie has a lot of respect for me, so I'm hoping he will come through for me and not lose it.)

"Yeah, maybe," was all I say in reply. "Let me know if you hear from him."

"Okay, later."

"Later, dude."

A few days later I get an e-mail from my brother. It was short and to the point, as most of his e-mails (and devoid of all proper grammer and punctuation). All it said was, "willies in jail."

I try calling the county jail to see if Willie is there. Wow, is that an automated run around; there is absolutely no option to talk to a real person. But after a couple tries, guessing which buttons I should push – what area I want to get to in their automated system to see if Willie is even there – I find out that he was released on April 15. Good news, I thought. So I wait to hear from him.

A week or two more passes and my brother finds out, through a pastor at a church Willie has been going to, that Willie *was* released, but he was released from jail and sent to prison. Willie is in the Racine Correctional Institution about two hours away, not easy visiting distance.

This only brings up a myriad questions for me: Why was Willie sent to prison? Was it for the same reason he was in jail or did he do something in jail that made them move him to a more secure, more severe facility? How long would this book project be put on hold, if we would be finishing it at all? It also started looking like I was going to have to cough up the money to replace the library's *Angela's Ashes* audio player.

Now that I know where Willie is really at, I decide I am not going to wait around for him to contact me; I have a time line on returning this audio book to the library, so I can't wait. I've been able to check it out for another few weeks, but the clock is ticking to the almost inevitable need to replace it.

I look the Racine facility up online and discover there are different units the inmates are housed in, and they have different visiting hours with different rules. I don't know where Willie is, so I decide to try and call. When I dial the number, I'm expecting the same mess of recorded messages that I received from the local jail. This time I actually get a real person! I explain that I'm a friend of Willie Triplett, and I'd like to contact him. She tells me he's in the Sturtevant Transitional Facility in the probation and parole unit. I ask if I can write him, and she gives me his DOC (Department of Corrections) number and housing unit number and a different address than is listed on the facilities website. I'm glad I had asked.

She also tells me that Willie has to put me on a visitor list before I can visit. That list has to be approved, then Willie will contact me to let me know I can come and see him.

I also explain that Willie has an audio book that belongs to my local library. She tells me to contact a different person and gives me their number. I call the number, and I am again surprised because it is an actual person's office number. She is not in, so I leave a message. Only a day later I get a message back telling me Willie did not bring anything with him to Sturtevant, that maybe I should check back with the local jail.

Oh great! I think. *The automated voice from hell.* I decide to bypass that route and drive down to the facility. I should be able to talk to a real person there, I think. I should!

A few days later I walk into the Dane County Jail and discover I was wrong. When I step into the lobby, I feel like I'm walking into a bad B movie; one of those movies where the actor opens a door only to find a small empty room and more doors.

The place is empty. The entryway is painted in shades of drab gray and is no bigger than twenty by twenty feet with a locked elevator on one side, some locked doors in front of me, and an empty security window and doors to my left. I walk a little further into a small foyer and find a short hallway to the right. I take it. It leads to another area with security windows that closes off a room that looks like it's set up for visitors, with round tables and chairs scattered around the room. The place is empty; no one is working at the window and no inmates or visitors are in the room. I'm in a major jail in the capitol city in Wisconsin and there is not a soul to be seen. Have I stepped into the *Twilight Zone*? It all just seems so bizarre.

I walk back into the main entrance and notice there is a doorbell button by the empty security window on the left side of the room. I go over and ring the bell. Halleluiah! A real person appears, and they're not dressed all in black or have black pencil all around their eyes like I'm expecting. Actually, the woman is quite pleasant, and I present my case.

"I have a friend that was here a while ago that has an audio book that belongs to the library," I say, thinking if I talk about what the library needs not what I need, I might get a better response. "I need to find out if it is still here."

"Sure. Just go through that door and up to the window, and they should be able to help you, she says, pointing to my left."

She buzzes me into a small room, again with multiple doors and a security window straight ahead of me. I walk up to the window. This room has a couple of tall file drawers and a rack like the one you would see attached to the ceiling in a drycleaners. It has neat looking clothes in plastic bags hanging all around it. I ask the man that steps up to the window about the audio book. It takes him a little while to find Willie's file, but it tells him that all his possessions where taken by a man named Mark.

"I think I know who that is," I say. (One of Willie's pastor friends, I hope.)

So I have another lead, and I am off to fight another day.

When I look back at the online information about Sturtevant, I realize my ability to see Willie is even more restricted than just by distance; visits are via television monitors and are limited to thirty minutes. Driving two hours for a thirty minute visit is just too impractical for me at the moment, so I decide I will write Willie a letter.

Dear Willie,

I'm sorry to hear that you are in prison. I would like to come visit you at some point, so you need to put me on your visitor list and let me know when they approve it. I'll ask Earl and my mom if they want to be on the list, too.

Maybe you can write down some things for the book while you're there and mail it to me. I have enclosed a self addressed stamped envelope to make it a little easier.

Also, I need to get that audio book "Angela's Ashes" back to the library. If you could let me know who has it, that would be helpful.

Take care of yourself and write back soon.

Christine

It takes a while, but I eventually get a letter back. It's written in very neat, feminine handwriting with punctuation this time, though not always correct.

House of Drugs

> *Dear Christiana, May 5, 2010*
>
> *What's up Christina?*
> *You put a very beautiful smile on my face, you made my day. I haven't been happy through all of this and yet I find that you sent me a letter. I couldn't receive the letter because you sent an envelope with the letter but I know you wrote and that made me happy. Im sorry the situation came about like this, I will keep working on my book while I am in here. I still have that Tape that you gave me, It's in my property. I think about you and your family and the book that we are putting together, You did tell me that you are my friend and Im happy that you meant it, I find it true. The reason Im in here is because I wrote the head program director to leave the program early, but they terminated me because they mistook the letter as that I wanted to quit when in fact I just wanted an early completion. I always will treat you like a lady becaue I feel you are a very beautiful lady, which is why I always treat you with respect. You can resent that the letter back to me, but please no extra envelopes inside. If that tape cost any money, I will pay it as soon as I get out. I am going to send you some stories from my book so you can write them for me when I get out.*

Then Willie proceeds to tell me about the first time he got high on cocaine. It was with a girl, of course.

He ends the letter as follows:

> *This is just a small taste of what I wanted to write down. I will with hold most of the graphic nature of the book until I hear from you, this is a small taste of what I intend to have put together. Somebody gave me this envelope so I wont be able to write you again until my P.O. send me my money so I can buy canteen, right now Im broke, but I buy envelopes when we are allowed to shop here. I will exlpain more about this in my next letter about jail and more story. I cant wait to here from you. Love your friend.*
> *Willie*

I find out later that Willie is in jail again because he didn't want to continue living in his present halfway house: the Schwert House. Let me explain why Willie was in this facilty in the first place.

On 8/13/09, seven months after Willie got out of jail for allegedly stealing someone's tools, Willie called his probation officer for help. (I say allegedly only because Willie told me that he was falsely accused of stealing. He was picked up and charged with the crime, but he said he didn't do it. He said a young woman, who Willie was getting high with, decided to press charges against him after he took some of her tools, tools that he said he returned to her after she had asked him to.) Why he got five years probation out of this,

I'm not sure. He was on probation for other crimes at the time that this happened, but five years seems excessive to me. But then what do I know.

Willie told his probation officer that he needed to be off the streets. He felt that he was "losing it" and needed treatment or revocation. He said if he had to, he'd stop seeing his PO (a condition of his parole) or do something else just so he could get picked up and given help. He told his PO "he needed to turn things around."

The PO called Willie back, and Willie told him he had used cocaine and drank. Willie wanted inpatient treatment because when he was working and getting paid, he used his money to get high and drink. Willie was told to report to the PO's office where he was served with revocation papers.

As an alternative to being put back in jail, they wanted to put Willie in a temporary living placement – a halfway house – but no halfway house was available at the time, so Willie was put back in jail. I don't know if the jail was full, or that the police realized that Willie really did need treatment and not jail time, but on 10/21/09 they let Willie out of jail because, according to Willie, they thought it was doing him more harm than good. They required Willie to report daily to the Day Report Center and restart treatment.

This plan worked for a time, but in mid-November Willie stopped showing up at the Day Report Center. He finally reported back in on 11/18/09 intoxicated and was again taken into custody and his parole revoked. In mid-December a halfway house, called the Schwert House, became available and Willie agreed to go. When he was at the Schwert House, Willie was required to look for a job each day, which meant going to various businesses and asking them to sign a paper saying he was looking for work. I'm not sure Willie was actually looking for work. He could have been; he really does enjoy working, but I was interviewing him during this time period, and I know he wasn't finding work other than the odd jobs my family or others were able to give him.

As time went on at the Schwert House, Willie got into some arguments with the staff. Eventually, Willie asked to leave the house, even though he only had two months left out of the four he was required to serve. He wasn't getting along with the staff and he wanted out early. He kept writing the staff up for things he thought they were doing wrong. What he got instead was put back in jail and eventually sent to prison. Willie couldn't stay in the Dane County Jail because, according to Willie, Racine was a parole holding location for the state, so it was cheaper to keep him there than in Madison.

Willie has a revocation hearing set for 5/25/10. This is where Willie first meets Mike – the lawyer that he is given by the state. Mike presents Willie's case and the judge sides with Willie, that he shouldn't be in prison, and Willie is released from jail June 6.

Chapter 14
Revocation of parole, again

Fast forward to January, 2011, after Willie's out of Strudevant prison in Racine for the second time.

"So what happened? Why were you picked up again?"

Willie somewhat sheepishly hands me his revocation summary. He has asked for all of his paperwork so that he can give it to me for his book. The man is thinking.

(I have changed the names to initials, otherwise this is unchanged from the original document.)

"At approximately 6:37pm, Officer R. and I were dispatched to Shopko. . . Dispatch advised Loss Prevention Officer T.H. was calling reporting a subject inside the store attempting to pass counterfeit $100 bill. Dispatch provided a description of the suspect inside the store and advised he was currenly near checkout lane #1. Both officers responded to the store and a short time later we arrive on scene.

CONTACT WITH TRIPLETT

Upon arrive both R. and I walked inside Shopko store. Upon entering the store, I observed a subject matching the description of the suspect for this case. The suspect was exiting the store as we were entering. Both R. and I began to talk with this subject about what he was doing at Shopko store. Triplett told us he was trying to purchase a PS3 player for some friends. Triplett stated he was in the parking lot of Shopko and three people approached him in a green colored vehicle. Triplett said it was occupied by three black males. When asked if he could provide a description he couldn't. Triplett said he was given $400 dollars to go inside the store and buy a PS3 player. Triplett further stated once he purchased the PS3 player the three males would give him $50 for his service. Officer R. further spoke with Triplett while I entered the store and spoke with employees. See Officier R's supplemental report for further information.

CONTACT WITH H.

I went inside Shopko and spoke with H., the loss prevention officer for Shopko. H. told me one of the cashiers told him about a subject in her lane with possible counterfeit bills. The cashier told H. she used the counterfeit bill marker on the bill and on all four bills the marker indicated they were not real. H. said he verified this by looking at the bills. H. stated he immediately called the Monona Police Departemnt to have officers respond to the store. H. further stated the subject was attempting to purchase a PS3 player and did have a store tag with him when he approached the register indicating he wanted to purchase the PS3 player.

DETAINING TRIPLETT

Triplett was currently on probation. Dispatch made telephone contact with the afterhour's probation officer explaining to them the case. Dispatch advised the probation officer has never had a case such as this one and would have to make telephone contact with their supervisor. While we were waiting for confirmation Officer R. conducted a pat down search of Triplett. Triplett told us he had a crack pipe in his front shirt pocket. Officer R. did locate a pipe in the front left chest pocket of Triplett. This was later placed into a brown paper bag and I took possession of the pipe. Triplett was handcuffed by Officer R. We escorted Triplett to the rear passenger seat of my patrol squad where he was secured.

While Triplett was in the back seat of my squad he contined to make statements such as, that was fucking stupid of me, man what was I thinking, god damn, fucking stupid shit.

I transported Triplett to the Dane County Jail giving dispatch my beginning and ending miles at the jail. Once at the Dane County Jail I parked in the sally port and removed the handcuffs from Triplett. I told Triplett to remain in the back seat while I was standing on the outside of the vehicle with the rear door open.

Willie Lee Triplett

FURTHER QUESTIONING OF TRIPLETT

I read Triplett the constitutional rights verbatim off a constitiutional rights notification card that I keep on my person. I asked Triplett if he understood these rights and he stated he did. I asked Triplett realizing he had these rights if he was willing to answer my questions or make a statement. Triplett wanted to know what questions I had for him, and I told him I may get to those questions once he answered the question. Triplett stated he would answer my questions.

I asked Triplett where he got the counterfeit money. Triplett continued with his initial statement of how three males approached him and offered to give him $50 for his service. I asked Triplett where he was going to sell the PS3 player at once he purchased it. He stated he wasn't he was going to give to those guys. I further asked Triplett why he wouldn't have just taken the money and ran and not return with a PS3 player. Triplett stated because he wanted the $50. I asked Triplett so you knew the money wasn't real money. Triplett turned his head away from me and stated he didn't know. I told Triplett I didn't believe his story because I could tell he was lying to me. Triplett said believe what you want to believe I know the truth. I asked Triplett what he was going to use with the $50. He stated drugs. I again asked Triplett why he wouldn't have used the $400. Triplett said he was using that for the PS3 player. I informed Triplett if he told me where he got the counterfeit money from I may look at trying to help him out. Triplett stated he didn't need any help. At this time Triplett stated he wanted to go inside the jail and didn't care to talk with me any further."

Chapter 15

The Hearing

Willie finally gets a hearing about his case. It's at the Dane County Court House. One of the Pastors Willie knows and Willie's lawyer both had left me a message that Willie would like me to be at the hearing. The lawyer, Mike, and I exchanged a few voice mails before we finally were able to talk. He said that Willie wanted me to write him a letter of recommendation, so to speak, but Mike didn't think it was necessary. The pastor had already done this, and Mike thought that would be sufficient. I didn't write the letter.

I live in Dane County so it is easy for me to show up at the court house. I forget that I would be going through a metal detector, so my Swiss Army knife is confiscated at the doors. (Unlike at the airport, I did get it back when I left.)

The court house is quite a bit more hospitable than the jail just next door, with big windows, polished metal elevators, and light wood paneled walls in the hallways and inside the courtrooms.

There are three or four rows of bench seats in the courtroom I step into. I sit in the back. Another man dressed in street clothes is in front of me. We are the only other people in the gallery. There are few people mulling around doing things in front of us.

A man in a suit and tie comes in and shakes hands with the man a few rows ahead of me. This is Willie's court appointed lawyer – Mike, the same man Willie had used when he wanted to leave the halfway house after he had gotten out of jail. When he knew he was going back to court, he wanted this same lawyer to represent him again. Soon after, the judge and a few other people appear and Willie is lead into the room. He's wearing an orange jump suit. He doesn't see me sitting in the darkened gallery.

The proceeding starts, most of which I can't understand, and eventually Willie stands to make a statement. Willie is very polite and he sounds sincere in his statement of guilt, stating how he wants to improve himself and do better if he is allowed to be released.

The whole thing is over in less than twenty minutes. The lawyer and the man in front of me turn to leave. This is the first time I am introduced to Pastor Paul. The lawyer also introduces himself. I am told that Willie will get six months in prison and five years probation. I am not sure if this is exclusively for Willie's last offenses (at Shopko) or if his prior parole revocation issue is in there, too. I don't know the system well enough to have the answer, and I don't want to waste Mike's time asking him. Mike tells me Willie has had already done two and a half years probation total, so when he gets out, he'll have one and a half years probation left.

Eventually I get a letter from Willie tucked inside a thank-you card. Willie is writing me from New Lisbon Correctional Institution where he has been sent. The beginning of the letter is in Willie's flowing script, the majority of it is not. The portion of the letter Willie dictates uses language that obviously is not his own.

> Date is 2011
>
> Today is Sunday night. I am look at the ~~muise~~ America muis ~~w, awad~~ award. Sit her think about my life. How I feel in side, about me. I feel I am a loser in life and my ~~spirst~~ spirit. I hate me for do drug in my life. I am hurt in my heate abot me doing drug.
>
> I solved the problem with me cellie by moving to another cell. Being in Dogde, and then here, Ive noticed Ive changed a little bit. Some things I feel like a man should stand up for himself. Like fighting to defend territory and boundries.

Being in Wisconsin it seems that fighting is not the correct course, unlike Illinois where it really is the only course accepted. I feel that being in Wisconsin the system is set up for "stool pigeons" as they would be called in Illinous. It hurts to feel this way, that the way it being set up here is so different so that I can't fight the system and I feel guilty for it. Yesterday around 7pm the music awards came on. I sit back watching other guys watching T.V. There were about 10 of us. I was at the same time reflecting on my life and how I wasted it with drinking and drugs. I wonder what could have come of my life without drugs and alcahol. Also what a difference I would have made to others had I not made the decisions I did...

I felt so bad watching the music awards on Sunday. It made me feel worthless and helpless. Almost as if I would want to hurt myself because of the feeling.

Tuesday I noticed that everyone was excited for Thanksgiving. Every inmate was getting ready with their canteen to cook a Thanksgiving dinner. Everyone is calling their families. <u>Alot</u> of inmates made a big canteen order. Most were waiting on the big football game ... We got a Thanksgiving day "brunch" today, but it wasn't anything like *what anyone in the world out there would really call a decent brunch. All we get special for dinner tonight is going to be a singe slice of pumpkin pie. This will be my first (and last!) time in prison in Wisconsin. For those guys I see in here doing a life sentence today is just another day to them.*

Today is Thursday, yesterday I got something in the mail I had a phone conversation from my P.O. at about 9 or 9:30 am. I was in the room with the social worker and the unit manager. The office was about 20 square foot large, with a desk in the center, fronted by the chair I sat in. To the right, along the wall was a counter on which were lots of files and papers. A computer sat in front of her and there were several inspirational pictures and poster on the wall along with a dry-erase board on which was written encouraging and positive things. The unit manager sat with me, on my left, which the social worker sat across the desk in front of her computer, by the phone. She dialed to Madison and put the conversation on the speaker with my P.O. We talked about the rules I had to [follow], school, meetings, what made me relapse last time, and my housing living arrangements I had planned. We agreed that I would be able to move in with Dave upon release. They want to put

> *me on a bracelet. And electronic monitoring device that tracks when I come and go from my house and relays that to my P.O. by land-line phone. I wear the bracelet on my ankle and a base device sits connected to my home phone at all times.*

On a separate, smaller white piece of paper Willie notes:

> *The P.O. asked me a series of questions designed to determine if I need to be placed on electronic monitoring. After we finished he told me that I did not need to be placed on the bracelet upon my release... I hope everything is going well for you and your family. I sent your mother a get well card about her knee. I also spoke to her on the phone. I hope she is doing wonderful. I'm doing good myself. This piece of paper is from the pad I got in Dodge that I forgot to send to you before. I love you and your family and I hope you all have a wonderful holiday.*

The thank-you card says: *Thank you very much! Your loving friend, Willie.*

December, 2011

I'm taking a trip to New Lisbon, Wisconsin to Lisbon Correctional Institution. New Lisbon is a town of 2,500, and the prison is just outside of town, just off the interstate. I pull up to a small parking lot and a rather non-descript, small, one-story building constructed of light-colored brick and enclosed in fencing – all but the entrance. This is how everyone goes in and out of the prison. The prison housing units are in a separate building behind this one. New Lisbon is a medium security prison that has a total of eight buildings, two of which house the nine hundred and fifty or so inmates.

I had read on the Internet that I needed to bring an ID and a quarter to get in; the quarter is for a locker to put your things into: keys, purse, bra... Yes, bra – you cannot have anything with any metal in it, like an underwire bra. There is a woman in front of me that has to take her bra off for just that reason. They also have a dress code similar to what you might have in a high school: no shorts or skirts shorter than your finger tips when your arm is at your side, nothing that shows your midriff, nothing low cut. I'm not exactly sure why the need for the dress code, but I can guess.

The website also talks about bringing money in, quarters again, but I didn't understand those instructions until I get here and see a family that is checking in before me. They have a plastic bag full of quarters. Visitors are allowed to bring in fifteen dollars in quarters to use during the visit; the inmates are not supposed to handle the money, only the visitors. They can use the money for vending machines, to buy food that other inmates make (bars, cookies, cake...), or buy items that the inmates make (hand painted pictures, crocheted hats or scarves, handmade toys...). The inmates have their own money for things like getting a haircut, which is another thing that fellow inmates provide. As I sit and wait, I wish I'd have understood those online instructions so I could have brought Willie a few dollars that he could spend while we visited.

After I show my ID and take all the stuff out of my pockets, including my car keys, and put it all in a locker, I am approved to visit. I get an invisible stamp on my hand (just like for getting into a bar event). I go through a metal detector, through a couple locked and secured doors (doors that open electronically when they unlock it for you) to an outside fenced in area about the size of a small dog enclosure. This is outside the housing units. The whole prison in total takes up one hundred acres. In front of me is the one-story concrete prison surrounded by approximately fifty feet of lawn. The lawn is surrounded by a set of very tall fences, the outside one topped with razor wire. Willie said the inside one was electrified. I don't remember seeing signs to that effect, but I guess Willie would know.

I am again let through two locked fence doors and walk outside toward the housing units. I can see a small, maybe thirty by one-hundred foot exercise area fenced in next to the building a ways off.

I am told to follow the sidewalk to the housing building, as if I'd get a wild hair and decide to take a stroll around the grounds. I'm sure there is someone watching me, someone with a highpowered rifle, but I can't see them. I enter the building and have to show my hand under a black light before they will open another locked door into the visiting room.

I'm not sure I understand this hand stamp thing since I can't imagine anyone getting past the metal detector, four electronically controlled doors, and the barbed wire and electric fences. But I don't ask, not wanting to act like a smartass to the guards who don't appear to have a sense of humor, so I just keep my mouth shut.

I enter the room and check in with a guard who is sitting in a small area behind glass cases that display items for sale, items the inmates have made. The guard is sitting on a platform that places him above everyone else, I presume so he can keep a better eye on everyone. Everyone has to check in with this man when they enter this common room, even the prisoners. I tell him I'm here to see Willie Tripplet, and he instructs me to sit at a specific numbered table.

Besides the shelves and display cases, there are rows of numbered tables in the room, approximately twenty square tables that seat four people and two tables that seat eight. There are a smattering of people in the room; the inmates can be pick out by their blue pants. Interestingly to me, most of the people in the room are white, either Caucasian or Hispanic. There are only a handful of black people. It's not what I expected.

I sit at my assigned table and wait, taking in the rest of the room since I don't have anything else to do. I am sitting in front of a row of vending machines facing into the room. The vending machines are pretty popular. Now I know where all those quarters go. There is also a microwave because you can buy hamburgers and other food items out of the vending machines that need to be heated. There are also the usual snack foods and sodas. There is a men's and women's bathroom to my left and another guard sitting in front of a computer on a platform against the wall to my right. Behind him are two large windows that look into a room that appears to be the chapel; I can read a few bible passages on a sign on the wall. Next to this other guard is an inmate selling the baked items I mentioned. This is pretty popular, too.

I sit quite a while because I find out, after Willie shows up, that he had been sleeping. He said he hadn't slept well last night, so he was taking a nap. When Willie shows his smiling face in the glass of a door in the far right side of the room, the guard in front of the chapel gets up and goes in to meet him. Willie has to spread his arms (and I suppose his legs – the door obscures the lower half of his body), so the guard can search him before he gets let into the common room.

Willie smiles at me and struts over to the guard by the for-sale items. He checks in with him before he comes over to me.

Willie gives me a nice, brotherly hug.
"So how you doin', sister?"
"I'm good. How are you?"
"I'm good."

"How's the writin' going? (Willie always wants to know how I'm doing with his story.)

"It's going kind of slow. I have another small story I'm working on that I'd like to get out before Christmas."

"Well, you can put this in there," he says, jesturing to the room."

(I plan on it.)

"So how is this place different than Dodge?" I ask.

"At Dodge I was locked up for twenty-three hours a day. I was in maximum security 'cause of my violent past record. Here is kind'a laid back. You free to go wherever you want. But you get free time to get outta your cell if you do classes or church. The courtyard's open eight in the mornin' to eleven at night."

"So are you doing any classes?"

"Doin' drug and alcohol programs. And programs to help to get a job, bank account. . . It's a tax money scam. First of all, alotta people been through dat – classes like dat. The tax payer people pay for it, to rehabilitate dat person. You gotta rehabilitate yourself. The inmates, dey don't care. Only people in dere responsible is the officer."

"How's the food?"

"The food sucks! It ain't no real food no more – soybean and stuff. Gotta have real meat. All soybean do is make you fat. Dat why dey got a commissary [where the inmates could buy other food].

"It's the same food prepared the same way, no salt, no nothin'. You know how dey fix old folks food? Dat's how dey fix it. You know some guys have bad health. Dey make everyone eat it."

"I read in your letter that they're going to let you live with Pastor Paul when you get out. That's nice."

"Yeah. He came once or twice ta visit."

"How was the prison in Illinois different than this one?"

"In New Lisben, the po-lices run dis. In Illinois, the prisoners run dat. Dey see and dey don't see. See, it's more violent in Illinois. The po-lice get involved if dere's a war, but not with the small stuff. But dat was back in the day. It might be different now."

I find out that sometime after my visit that Willie was sent to "the hole" – where you're locked down for twenty-three hours a day. He was there because he didn't like the way another prisoner was "takin' smack" to him.

He describes the incident to me.

"Dis guy come over and tried to talk shit. Sayin' how he got dis and dat. He say he ain't lyin'.

"I say, 'You talkin' all dat crap. You ain't even got a TV in your cell. You ain't got money.' I don't wanna hear dat shit. He get real loud. The po-lice told us to hold it down. The guy keep on talkin' shit.

"Every Tuesday in Wisconsin, everyone go home [whosever scheduled to go home]. He was goin' to the county jail [that next Tuesday]. He try and make a way dat I don't get out. See, you ain't guaranteed you gonna get out.

(That pissed Willie off that this guy would suggest that Willie wouldn't get out of prison; a sore topic for any inmate.)

"He throw water on me. So I hit 'im in the jaw so it don't show no bruise. If I hit him in the eye, dey could'a give me more time.

"I had a hearin'. Dey found me guilty. Dey give me a hundred fifty days in the hole. We bof' went to the hole. He got out dat Tuesday [because he was scheduled to leave the prison that day]. If he had bruises, dey could'a pressed charges, but it was just another fight. He ain't hurt."

"Why did he throw water on you?"

"I was callin', his bluff. I say, 'You ain't nobody. You always talkin' shit. You say you got all dis stuff.' He say he's makin' $200,000 a year.

"I say, 'You makin' more den the officer here. Why ain't you get a lawyer to get you out?'"

Willie only served twelve of his one hundred and fifty days in the hole because he was scheduled to leave on the 24 of January.

Chapter 16
Willie's Out

~~~~~~~~

I meet with Willie at my brother's house. He's helping him paint the inside of his house, and whenever Willie is working, he likes to make me his excuse for having to stop and take a break.

Willie greets me with his now usual brotherly hug and a "How you doin'?" Willie's bright-eyed today. He just woke up from a short nap that he took after his lunch while he was waiting for me to arrive.

I ask him how it's going living with Paul.

"I ain't livin' dere right now.

"I was out of my meetin' [AA]. I was cookin' a sausage. The wife axed me not to do dat because she didn't want people she had invited over to smell dat. She said, 'Please don't cook.'

"She did it once before, axed me not to cook breakfast. She don't like the smell of bacon in her house. Dey had alotta rules."

"What does Paul say about you moving out?"

"I met with him yesterday. I might go back tomorrow.

"She wanted to show off to all her friends her new kitchen. Her husband try to talk to her about it.

"He axed me, 'Why don't you just come on back?' I don't want to walk on egg shells, or I don't want *her* to walk on egg shells.

"I'm thinkin', be honest with me. Just be honest with me. What if God would'a told her, no? What Jesus went into the world for? I say to myself, I don't have to take dat shit. I left and stayed at the shelter a couple days. I went and got some suggestions from a couple people. My thinkin' is, you want me to cook, den you turn around and say no. I shouldn't have been in dat situation. It's my own fault for bein' in dat situation. Her husband see more in me. He see the progress dat I'm doin'. It come down to my reality. She so comfortable in her life, she never lose somethin'.

"I tell him, 'I don't want you and your wife to get in a big argument.' He say everythin' cooled off. He say it's okay, but the tension still dere. You can just tell. Guys know women have mood swings.

"She hurted my feelin's. You welcome me but you might not like me dere. Me and her husband hang out a lot. When I go rent a movie on Saturday and Sunday, I watch movies all day. He come down and watch a couple movies with me. She prob'bly used to him always dere. Dey married for thirty years. Womans like attention, some guys do, too.

"He begged me to come back. I planned to be out a whole week; give dem a breather. Yesterday I bought me some underwear and socks so I could take me a shower at the shelter: shelter two. Shelter one is where dey check you out – you take a breathalyzer. Dey get you up at five o'clock, and dey want you out by six o'clock. Dey have cereal. I don't do cereal. I can't eat dairy, it give me gas and diarrhea, so I get somethin' else.

"Eight-thirty the shelter open [shelter two]. Staff came at eight fifty-five.

"He say, 'What time you get here? [The man running the shelter.]

"'I got here ten minutes ago.'

"He poked at me for some reason. [The man at the shelter was trying to get Willie worked up.] He tried to talk shit, to make a big argument to kick me out. He say, 'Come and get it,' like Tyson. I don't do like I usually do. I told his supervisor instead'a gettin' mad.

"He said, 'Go ahead.'

"I told him I called the supervisor boss.

"I say, 'I feel dat one of your staff talk to me in a wrong manner, and I took dat as a threat.'

"He should be fired, not written up. Not being professional in dis type of field, of what he do. I left a message. I called back to find out he a volunteer from Christ Lutheran in Fitchburg.

"I got up at five a.m. I brushed my teeth. Dey got carpet. Dey have mats and a blanket. Dey wash the blanket once a month. Dey check you in, den you get a blanket and a mattress. Dey use dat place not only for a shelter but for a drop-in center. It give you a place to go, get out the cold. Dey use dat for a different organization, too. The homeless sleep dere at night.

"I walked to McDonald's to have breakfast, me and one other guy. He was in New Lisbon prison. He kind'a crazy. He had twenty years. He was a 3rd degree child molster: his step daughter. He was tellin' me he still got that crazy mentality for young womens. I told him why don't you go buy a woman? He said she came onto him. I think he came onto her. I don't really feel sorry for him. My sister got raped, so I didn't feel sorry for him. In Chicago you get killed or get raped for dat.

"I bought him a breakfast, just bein' a human bein'."

"Are you gonna work for the ashpalt guy this summer?"

"I done had dat job for ten years. I was doin' good for three years. The reason dey keep hirin' me back 'cause God gave me dat job. The daddy likes me. [The man who runs the company.] The mother don't like me. She say, 'You always get things'. He see dat. He payin' more attention to what I'm doin'. His brother goin' through dis. The daddy got a back problem. He take alotta pills, but he know how to take care of his business. His son do what his dad do. Some'a the people I know dere, dey do drugs, takin' pills. Some get up and go to work, a functional addict. You can see dey have a hangover the next day.

"Addicts, dey don't wanna stop, but dey losin' alotta things. The other part of the addiction tell them it feel good. Dey control deir addiction, same as Whitney Huston. She didn't find a hobby. She should of gone back dere, go back to church. She start at church. She get depressed. Her addiction tell her, go get drugs. You sneakin' it. Your addiction don't care. Put you back in dat state, in relapsin'. It's hard. Once you taste dat clean and sober, it feel good. She relapsed so bad.

"God can give you all the signs in the world, but are you payin' attention? Anythin' can be your God. Den you got to find a way to stop."

"Are you goin back to school?"

"I am in October. I gotta get my stuff together, get some money, get a place to live."

"How's it going with your probation officer?"

(Willie hasn't had the best track record with probation

officers. Sometimes Willie doesn't like to follow rules, particularly if they seem unnecessary to him or as least inconsequential. We have that in common.)

"He tryin' to make me pay some money, a probation fee. Go see what I owe, but I gotta get money for a place to stay and for school."

"You think he's pocketing that?"

"No he ain't. It go somewhere. He found out what I owe. He go on the big computer. He say, 'You don't owe no money.'

"Dey took five hundred and eight dollars [his 2010 tax check] – the probation agent people – and dey say I owe a probation fee before I go to Racine, and the state take it.

"He say, 'You don't know what will come down the line.' He afraid dey would start axin' me to pay again, another probation fee.

"I asked, 'Can I get off probation early?'"

"He say, 'No.'

"Dey told me dat you can; the DA told me.

"He try and keep me in the system. I got a year and a half."

"Why does he care?"

"Den he lose a job. Dey don't wanna let you off. It's easy money. It's a business. It's a hustle. Dey just use a bigger word for it.

"I see my probation officer once a month. In ninety days I can ask for two months dat I see him. He don't know dat I know dese things.

"How you beat 'em? you gotta think. When you drinkin' and druggin', you don't think. You start payin' attention. Your rest broken; you ain't gettin' enough rest. You constantly pushin' it. You cannot think. You see but you cannot hear. Your mind is so set in dat behavior. But when you ain't doin dese things, you can take the time to rest.

"I didn't sleep too well last night. My rest broken. I came here at seven a.m. and I sleep right away. My body is rested, and I can go at a normal pace. My mind been playin' dat situation. If I rest proper, I get up at seven to nine at night. If you don't rest, you can go back into dat behavior."

CHAPTER 17

Willie is Always Surprising Me

~~~~~~~~~~

I pick up Willie on his birthday to take him out to lunch and to teach him how to use a hand-held recorder. He's found a recorder, and he wants me to teach him how to use it. (I find out later it's his fiftieth birthday.) He's painting the outside trim of someone's home. Willie gets off his ladder when he sees me pull up.

"Hey, sister. What's up?"

"Not much, Willie. Happy birthday, by the way!"

Willie comes close like he's going to hug me but realizes he's all full of paint. We bump elbows instead, chuckling.

"So you able to stop?" I ask.

"Sure! I just got to put dis paint away and wash my hands."

Willie goes behind the house and comes out with what appears just as much paint on his hands as he had before. Maybe he wiped them off but he didn't wash them. He gets in the car.

"So where do you want to go for lunch?" I ask.

"Dere's dis place on Willie Street dat has really good Gyros."

"Gyros? I haven't had a Gyro in a long time" (probably over five years ago, in fact). "Sure."

So we head out.

Willie directs me to the place, and I start looking around for a parking spot on the street. He points to a gravel lot behind a home across from the restaurant. He assures me I won't get a ticket, but I'm still not sure. Willie hasn't had a driver's license in years, but I know he looks out for his friends, so I give up and park there, anyway. I don't see any parking signs, so I'm guessing that he might be right. We walk to the restaurant and sit at the bar. Willie doesn't go to the bathroom and wash his hands here, either. We both order a Gyro and fries and we wait for our food to come.

"So you have a recorder?" I ask.

"Yeah," he says and pulls a small digital recorder out of his pocket.

"Did you borrow this?" ("Borrowing" something is Willie-speak for stealing.)

He chuckles. "No. I found it."

I believe him because Willie isn't shy about telling the truth when it comes to "borrowing." He doesn't see anything wrong with it. I make a mental note to ask him sometime why that is.

I play with the recorder and can't really figure it out, so I excuse myself and go to my car for my recorder and the birthday presents I have brought along. I anticipated having trouble with his recorder, even though he assured me it was just like mine. I come back and set a small, soft-sided cooler in front of him on the bar.

"What's dis?"

"It's your birthday present."

Willie opens the cooler to find two packages of wrapped venison, something he has been asking me for for some time and in his usual Willie style, if he wants something, he just asks for it. I've also given him some sweetcorn we froze last year and some frozen garden tomatoes.

"Well, dat's so nice!" he says and means it.

I also pull out a gift card to Best Buy.

"That's so you can buy a movie," I say.

"I could'a used dat the other day. I was buyin' headphones."

"Well, now you can use it to buy a movie for your new TV."

A couple other friends of Willie's got together and bought him a new flat-screen TV for his new apartment.

Willie then went out and bought himself a DVD player, because Willie loves movies. Though he later admits to me that mostly "the movies watch me." He has been working so hard at his road construction job the last few weeks, he just lies down on the couch – which is his current bed – to watch a movie at the end of the day and ends up falling asleep because he is so tired.

Our food comes and we start eating. Somehow we get on the conversation of women, and I realize the woman Willie is complaining about is someone he has seen since he's gotten out of prison. I'm surprised he's hooked up with someone so quickly, though I shouldn't be.

"Where'd you meet her," I ask.

"On the bus."

That doesn't surprise me either. Willie will start up a conversation with anyone, anywhere, particularly a woman.

"But she's was just a booty call, and she wanted to control me, and I ain't into dat," he tells me between bites of Gyro. "She don't wanna go ta school," he says, looking at me straight on."

This is really an interesting statement coming from Willie. Then he goes on to say how she doesn't have any goals. Now I'm really shocked. I find out the next day when I'm interviewing cupcake, my eight-six year old aunt for a different book that I am writing, that she has talked to Willie about the type of girls he should see. How he should look for a girl who has goals, who works, and who doesn't drink. I hear Willie saying these *same* things to me and I'm surprised. I'm thinking, *maybe this will work for him this time, just maybe*.

"Does she work?" I ask.

"No. She got two flat screen TV's. She gets a welfare check, a check for child support, and she only pay 'bout fifty dollars for rent, and she say she's poor. Den she's talkin' to me about wantin' ta get her nails done," he says with disgust. "Like she want me ta pay for it!" His voice goes up a few octaves.

For a guy who is presently busting his butt working every and any job he can find to pay for the rent on his new apartment, the things he needs for his new cat (which I just find out he has), and his own food, he feels the indignation of the situation with the new girlfriend. He mumbles something about not staying with her, so I let the topic drop.

We finish our meal and head out. In Willie style he tells me (doesn't ask me) that he's got to stop at the cat store to buy cat litter for his cat. It has started raining now, so I tell him I can also take him to my mother's – his current *inside* paint job – because it's on my way to my work.

We stop by his apartment so he can drop off the things that my husband and I have given him for his birthday and so he can change his cat's litter box. It's kind of a funny coincidence. His apartment is exactly where the character in the current book I am working on is living: above the Crystal Corner Bar, though my character is living there in 1946. I am really curious as to what it looks like, so I ask if I can come up and see it. Willie agrees.

I find out it probably has changed a lot since 1946. There are three apartments where before it was remodeled there was maybe one or at most two. But Willie's apartment is just right for him: a one bedroom for five hundred dollars a month. Pretty reasonable as rentals go. Part of the cheap rent is that the bar has live music most Friday and Saturday nights. Luckily for Willie, he manages to sleep right though it.

"Dis is Taz," he tells me when we're greeted by a small black cat as we enter the apartment. He has to say it twice before I understand him, and he explains; it's short for Tasmanian devil.

"It's very friendly," I say as the cat repeatedly rubs up against my leg, purring away.

There are things strewn everywhere in the apartment. Not a real mess, but it's not clean, either, though he actually has a broom and dustpan sitting in his small kitchen. He points out the couch and matching chair he has in his living room and his prized flat screen TV.

"Where'd you get the furniture?" I ask.

"From someone at the church."

I look in the bedroom and there is another television, a standard TV, on the floor and some other debris. I have to get going to work, so I suggest I put his birthday food in his refrigerator. There is one plate and one cup in the drying rack next to the sink. I open the freezer to put his food in and it is empty. I remember the set of dishes I put in our attic recently, in case one of my children might want them at a later date. I make a mental note to give Willie a few of those dishes for his surprise birthday party this coming weekend.

"I don't cook 'cause I ain't got no fry pan or plates or anything," he tells me.

I help him dump his old litter into the garbage and we head out.

I'm about to turn the car around to head to my mother's but he explains, "We got to go back to the house [the house where I picked him up], 'cause the paint's still outside."

Again he tells me and doesn't ask. I call work and tell them I am going to be fifteen minutes late.

"You got a key to the Old Girl's house?" he asks.

"She's eighty-two, Willie. Of course I've got a key."

I open the house and he directs me to go in first. Willie is always the gentleman. I hear him mumble something behind me as he walks in.

"What did you say?" I ask.

"I just said 'Bless dis house,'" he explained.

"Really? Why did you say that?"

"Dat's what the Bible say. I always do dat."

I come in and check out what he's done so far with his paint work; he's doing a nice job, as usual. I leave the house a bit nervous that I'm leaving him alone. But mostly I'm still shaking my head in disbelief about his habit of blessing a house as he enters it. I am amazed at how Willie is always full of surprises.

CHAPTER 18

WiLLie's BiRTH-DaY

~~~~~~~~

I get a phone message from my brother that we are invited to a surprise party for Willie's birthday. It's at Pastor Paul's house. My brother is going to be there, and he'll bring our mother – the Old Girl. Closer to the party, my mother tells me the same thing, plus my Aunt Kay will also be going. She gives Willie a lot of work, so they know each other well. I plan on going, too.

The day arrives and I show up at Pastor Paul's house. It's in an older neighborhood in the city with older homes and well established trees. I don't see many cars, but as I walk up to the house, I see Pastor Paul. I recognize him from the courthouse, so I know I'm in the right place.

Willie's not here yet, so I meet and get to know some of the other people in Willie's life, most of whom, at this party, anyway, are from the church Willie attends, which includes Paul and his wife. I also find out that Paul is not a Pastor. In the typical Willie style, he has nicknamed him "Pastor Paul," just as he tried to nickname me cupcake – glad that's gone! – then pumpkin – better but still not what I'd prefer, and now sister – much better, especially considering the connotation that goes along with it. I note that there is only one other person who isn't white in this group. Willie actually invited someone he knows from the street, another black man. Even though it was to be a surprise party, Willie knew about it, but that person didn't make it.

When Willie finally arrives, he actually *is* surprised. He assumed there was going to be a party for him, even though Paul had just invited him over for dinner, but he didn't know all these people were going to be here. He is particularly surprised by my presence, which he comments on a few different times. I guess he felt I was too busy to come into town on a weekend for something like this. I'm kind of amazed by this. I guess he doesn't understand that I wouldn't be spending all of this time with him and my own money on this project if I didn't care about him and about his success. Willie and I are not close; I don't spend free time with Willie other than if he comes to my mother's for a meal or for some other celebration, but that doesn't mean I don't care about him or that, in a small way, Willie's struggle with sobriety is my struggle, as well. I'm hoping he realizes that, like me, all these people are here because they are all behind him, all rooting for him, all hoping that he can make it. In case he misses the point, at a later time in the party, Paul tells him just that.

I would guess Willie understands that getting this book out there, even if he makes any kind of money selling it, is not really germane to him staying clean and sober. I think it will boost his self-esteem. I think it could put him in the public eye, talking the talk. But will this help keep him away from drinking or drugs? It *might*, but Willie's been in it too long and addiction is too complex – a fact that Willie has tried to illustrate to us – for a mere book to keep Willie off the streets and out of jail.

Once Willie gets over the surprise of this whole party being in his honor, I can tell he is feeling a bit awkward. Whether it's from being the center of attention or being one of only two black people at the party, it's hard to tell. But he puts on a good face and works the crowd, saying, "Hello," "How you doin?" to everyone and teasing the young kids in the group, most notably the girls.

Willie dressed up for the occasion. He has on a nice sweater, a pair of dress pants, and slightly worn dress shoes. Willie might dress this way for church, but I know my family has hardly seen Willie without paint on his hands or at least under his nails. The man cleans up well.

Eventually we all get our food and sit and converse.

House of Drugs

Willie snatches food here and there; he is still acting the man of the hour and making the rounds. Eventually, after the cake is served, Willie starts to open gifts. Most are practical things like clothes, pots and pans, dishes. He even gets some DVD's from Paul which are religious in nature. He jokes that maybe that is not his style of movie. If Willie is anything, he is honest, but he does couch the rejection with a joke and a smile, so all is forgiven.

People start to leave in drips and drabs, all coming by Willie to wish him well. It has been a nice party, and I think Willie does feel supported by all these people and loved.

But I have left the start of the meal until the end of this story because, for me, it speaks of the momentous struggle Willie and other addicts like Willie have with their addictions. And as in AA meetings, the meal starts with a prayer.

After sufficient mulling about, Paul calls for a prayer to be said before the meal begins, and Willie is to do the honors.

Now, I have never heard Willie pray before, so I didn't realize the eloquence he has in that department. Let me tell you, the man has had his ears open at church services and can rival any good Baptist preacher.

Willie's prayer consists of the usual thanks for all we have, and asking for guidance themes that many prayers have, plus some preacher-speak about who is The One, and The Only One who we need to rely on or can rely on.

It goes on like this for quite a while, at least longer than most white preachers I've ever heard, not to mention longer than any prayer I've heard at a social function such as this one, where prayers are usually shorter than normal if said at all.

He impresses my mother and my aunt, two very devout women. He impresses me, too. But I have to admit, I still am not a believer – not a believer that Willie actually, *truly* believes all the things he just preached to us this warm summer afternoon: that he has given it all up to someone else, given up his worries, his doubts, his constant struggle with addiction. I doubt this because I don't *see* it in him, and that worries me.

It worries me because I believe that truly knowing, truly believing in a power higher than himself, is the only way Willie can make it out of the pit or "hole," as Willie describes it, that has formed around him, formed by many of the things you have read in this book and many of the things he has not shared with anyone. He's just in there too deep.

I've seen this ability to let go, this inscrutable task of giving it up to someone or something else, first hand, with the native people of El Salvador.

I have worked closely and made friendships with some El Salvdorians on work trips I have taken to their country with my church. Some of these El Salvadorians had been captured and tortured, seen their loved ones tortured or taken way, never to be seen again, during the civil war that ravaged their country in the 1980s. But still these people could smile, still they could sing. It amazes me to this day. And the only power that I know of that can overcome that kind of darkness, that kind of fear, that kind of hate, is a power that we as humans do not generate on our own.

But then it doesn't really matter what I believe, does it. It only matters what Willie believes. I hear it on his lips, but I only see glimmers of it in his eyes.

But maybe that is how it starts, with glimmers, with faint, out of focus hints of what is possible. And with repetition, through his actions; through the actions of others towards him and with him; with the telling and retelling of what he can see himself becoming, the walls of that hole will start to crumble and fade from view. He gets to see that sobriety is a reality, a reality that maybe still has to be taken one day at a time but a reality none-the-less and one he can live with.

Because isn't that really the most important thing, what Willie has repeated again and again to me when we have met to put down his thoughts? That when it comes to sobriety, he has to learn to live with it, the realness of it, the boringness of it, the everyday of it, and sometimes the pure pleasure of it. He has to learn to make that his new reality, like we all do, how we all struggle with it, with life: one day (and sometimes one moment) at a time.

Good luck, Willie! There are a lot of people behind you.

ABOUT THE AUTHOR

Christine is a writer, reader, author, editor, book designer and publisher. She loves writing and helping others publish the book of their dreams through her publishing company: CKBooks Publishing. Her first book: *Rosebloom*, won a national IPPY award in 2008 for historical fiction, her 2014 book: *Will the Real Carolyn Keene Please Stand Up* was a finalist for a Midwest Book Award for historical fiction and her 2016 middle grade book: *Intrigue in Istanbul: An Agnes Kelly Mystery Adventure* won a 2016 Moonbeam Children's Award. Christine teaches classes at local libraries for both youth and adults and a youth writing and publishing summer school class in New Glarus, WI.

You can find all of Christine's books at: christinekelenybooks.com. This is also where you can sign up for her Reader's Group.

If you enjoyed this book, please leave a review on your favorite website. Christine and Willie would greatly appreciate it.

ABOUT WiLLie TRiPLeTT

Willie is living with his cat in Madison. He is still working at the asphalt company summers and doing home maintanence on the side, though he would prefer year-round employment to help him stay out of trouble. He has gotten his temporary driver's license and plans on going to school again in the fall of 2013 if he can. Unfortunately, just before we were set to publish Willie's book, he relapsed again after being clean for two years.

Willie's struggle to stay clean and sober continues.

www.ingramcontent.com/pod-product-compliance
Lightning Source LLC
Chambersburg PA
CBHW020107020526
44112CB00033B/1085